Instructor's Manual and Test-Item

# THE PERSONALITY PUZZLE

WITHDRAWN

Instructor's Manual and Test-Item File

# THE PERSONALITY PUZZLE

**David C. Funder**
University of California, Riverside

Test-Item File by
**Jana S. Spain**
High Point University

W • W • Norton & Company • New York • London

ISBN 0-393-97049-3 (pbk.)

W. W. Norton & Company, Inc., 500 Fifth Avenue, New York, N.Y. 10110
http://www.wwnorton.com

W. W. Norton & Company Ltd., 10 Coptic Street, London WC1A 1PU

1 2 3 4 5 6 7 8 9 0

# Contents

**Preface**

# Preface

## General Considerations

Teaching a course in personality psychology is a challenging assignment in several ways. First, although the topic touches on many issues that students find intrinsically interesting, it also includes a mass of historical and technical detail that can, if not handled carefully, hide the forest behind the trees. Second, the field includes historically important megatheories such as Freud's, philosophical perspectives such as existentialism, and empirical research on factor analyses of personality traits and cognitive processes in goal-setting. Tying these together into a coherent package that students find meaningful is no small task.

## Plan of the Manual

*The Personality Puzzle* emphasizes topics students are likely to find interesting, while at the same time providing a sophisticated and rigorous analysis of these topics. It covers both historically and philosophically important perspectives and modern research. But if this book is used as part of a personality course, it is the instructor who brings the content of the course to life. The purpose of this manual is to provide a bit of help.

For each chapter in the text, the manual begins with an outline and summary (both taken from the text itself). Then I provide a few comments on the content of the chapter from an instructor's perspective, offer some suggestions on how to teach this content, and point to the relevance between material in the chapter and the selections in the companion Reader, *Pieces of the Personality Puzzle: Readings in Theory and Research* (edited by Daniel J. Ozer and myself). Finally, I list some discussion questions that might be useful in a small class or in sections of a larger class.

This manual also includes questions for course exams. These could be used as is or adapted for a particular instructor's emphasis. The questions were written by Dr. Jana Spain of High Point University (North Carolina), a former graduate student of mine who was a teaching assistant in my personality course and has taught the course on her own for several years.

## Selling Personality Psychology

Before beginning with the chapter-by-chapter commentary, a few general remarks are in order. First, as emphasized in the Preface to the text, the principal aim of the personality course, as I teach it, is to persuade students that personality psychology matters. All too often we hear psychologists lament that the general public neither understands nor appreciates our field. The "person on the street" identifies psychology with clinical psychology and often sees it as so much witch-doctoring. The public does not understand that psychology is a field of science that gathers and analyzes data and tries to account for those data with rigorously developed theories.

But if that description of the public is true, who is at fault? Given the large number of students who enroll in college-level psychology courses, the only ones psychologists should blame for the public not understanding their field is themselves. This is our big chance. If we bore our students, bog them down in trivia, or talk over their heads, we should not be surprised if they decide our field is a waste of time and money. But, if we can engage them, show them what psychology can teach them about their lives, and excite them about the same issues that we find exciting, the results will be beneficial for both the students and for psychology.

This is what I mean when I say that the purpose of *The Personality Puzzle* is to sell psychology. This does not mean I wish to neglect an education in research methods, theoretical content, or empirical research. But if, at the end of course, the student does not understand why any of these are important, then it is not clear what he or she has really learned.

My first piece of advice, therefore, is to touch on the real-life concerns of your students with the material of this course whenever you can. The purpose is not to turn personality into a field of pop-psychology, nor to "dumb down" the course. Rather, it is to act on the knowledge that if college professors do not explain to their students why psychology is important, it is unlikely anybody else ever will.

## Other Matters

Two final comments. First, as is mentioned in the Preface, the coverage of the text is selective. Obviously, *The Personality Puzzle* is not one of those twelve-pound tomes that attempt to be encyclopedic in their coverage. I hope this fact has two advantages—the book might be a bit more readable than some of its hefty cousins and its selectivity opens many areas for instructor-developed lectures that will not overlap the book. For example, an instructor with a particular interest and expertise in the neo-Freudians or the modern cognitive approaches will find both represented in the book, but with much more left to offer to his or her students. I will point out other possibilities in the sections that follow.

Finally, this is an opinionated text. I did not take the plain-vanilla approach to textbook writing, which means that there is room for disagreement in many places. I would urge an instructor who thinks me wrong on a particular point to explain to his or her students just how and why. I would further urge such an instructor to be careful in how such disagreements are handled. I have found out—the hard way—that if I tell students that some other psychologist disagrees with me because that psychologist is ignorant or confused, students conclude that *everybody* in psychology is ignorant and confused. Although we psychologists are somewhat notorious for getting carried away in the heat of our disagreements with one another, the more objectively, analytically, and respectfully we can explain such disagreements to our students, the more likely they are to find the topics worth their own serious thought.

Instructor's Manual and Test-Item File

# THE PERSONALITY PUZZLE

# The Study of the Person

## Summary

Personality psychology's unique mission is to try to explain the psychological functioning of whole individuals. This is an impossible mission, however, so different approaches to personality must limit themselves in various ways. Personality psychology can be organized into five basic approaches: trait, biological, psychoanalytic, phenomenological, and behavioral. Each addresses certain aspects of human psychology quite well, and ignores others. The advantages and disadvantages of each approach seem inseparable. The book is grouped into five sections that survey each basic approach. Sometimes regarded as a demeaning attempt to pigeonhole people, personality psychology's real implication is an appreciation of the ways in which each individual is unique.

## About the Chapter

As introductory chapters go, this one is fairly brief. It introduces and defines personality, briefly, and explains that the topic is so broad it must be divided into five basic approaches. I group together the behavioral, social learning, and cognitive approaches into one, because (as will be seen later) I think the lineage and connection between them is clear. Some instructors might prefer to present six rather than five basic approaches, either by separating this last section into behavioral/social learning vs. cognitive, or behavioral vs. social learning/cognitive. (My own failure to decide which of these worked better is one reason why I combined all three.)

An important point emphasized throughout the book, and perhaps worth mentioning in lecture, is that the basic approaches (however one counts them) are not different answers to the same question, they are different questions. And it also might be worth mentioning the truism in science—which will be new to most students—that in research the questions are more important than the answers. Answers always change over time, while certain questions are eternal. The basic questions asked by the five (or six) approaches to personality may be among these.

The most unusual aspect of this chapter is probably its promise that personality psychology is interesting, and that the book will not bore them. This promise will not be fulfilled for all students (it is awfully hard to get certain students interested in anything), but I hope it works out for many. If nothing else, I hope students find it refreshing to see a text promise to try to be interesting, rather than take the attitude that "this is difficult material and if you find it boring, that's too bad." Please note that the chapter does not promise the material will be simple. Simple material is not often interesting, and the book that follows is not simple.

## Teaching Notes

One exercise I often do at the beginning of the course, before anything else, is to ask students this: If you could ask an expert who knew everything about human psychology one question, what would that question be? I have them write their responses, hand them in, and then I read a subset of them aloud (either right then or in the next class meeting). It is interesting to note that easily 70 to 80 percent of the questions students ask fall within the domain of personality psychology. This is a good way to make the points: (a) personality is at the center of what people ordinarily mean by the term "psychology," and (b) a course and book that covers questions like these ought to be interesting and valuable.

Then it is time to begin presenting course material. In my own course, I seem to present less introductory material every year. I find that few of the abstract, overview-type comments that I used to make meant anything to my students. In particular, I have found that the first (or second) day of the term is not a good time to compare and contrast alternative paradigms, comment on the place of personality psychology within the field as a whole, or editorialize about my favorite approach. Instead, I try to motivate their interest in the topic (as described above), and *briefly* outline and define the basic approaches to be covered. I also tell them, for the first of what will be many times, that the different approaches consist of different questions, not competing answers.

## Reader Notes

From Section I, the piece by Dan McAdams, "What do we know when we know a person," raises all the right issues for the beginning of a personality course. Of course, the best question he raises is the one in his title, which is another excellent topic for course discussion. One could have this discussion, based on the same question, on both the first *and* last day of the course. It would be fascinating to take notes on the first day and then compare what is said to the answers offered on the last day.

## Discussion Questions

1.  *What is the purpose of psychology? What kinds of questions should a science of psychology seek to answer?*
2.  *Why are you taking this course? What do you hope to learn? Of what use do you expect it to be?*
3.  *If you could choose what this course is to be about, what would you ask for? Why?*
4.  *Which is more important: answers or questions? (This discussion could lead into some*

*elementary philosophy of science with which an instructor so inclined could prepare students for material to come later in the course.)*

5.  *What do we know when we "know" a person?*

## Multiple-Choice Questions

1.  Personality is an individual's characteristic patterns of
    a. behavior.
    b. emotion.
    c. thought.
    d. all of the above

    Answer: d    Page: 1
    Topic: The Goal of Personality
        Psychology

2.  The unique mandate of personality psychologists is to attempt to
    a. identify and measure individual differences in ability and behavior.
    b. determine the effect of the social environment on behavior.
    c. explain whole, functioning persons in their social context.
    d. prevent or treat psychological personality disorders.

    Answer: c    Page: 2
    Topic: The Goal of Personality
        Psychology

3.  Personality psychologists who adhere to the _____ focus on identifying, conceptualizing, and measuring the ways

that people differ psychologically from one another .
a. psychoanalytic approachb. trait approach
c. cognitive approach
d. phenomenological approach

Answer: b    Page: 2
Topic: Mission Impossible

4.  Personality psychologists adhering to the _____ focus on psychic energy, the workings of the unconscious mind, and the nature and resolution of internal mental conflict.
a. psychoanalytic approach
b. trait approach
c. cognitive approach
d. phenomenological approach

Answer: a    Page: 2
Topic: Mission Impossible

5.  Psychologists following the phenomenological approach
a. focus primarily on the workings of the unconscious mind and the resolution of internal mental conflict.
b. study how our overt behavior is affected by rewards and punishments.
c. build theoretical models of how people process information.
d. are concerned with our conscious experience of the world and the consequences of having free will.

Answer: d    Page: 2
Topic: Mission Impossible

6.  The personality paradigm that focuses on rewards and punishments is the
a. trait paradigm.
b. behaviorist paradigm.
c. phenomenological paradigm.
d. psychoanalytic paradigm.

Answer: b    Page: 2
Topic: Mission Impossible

7.  _____ theories focus on how the basic processes of perception, memory, and thought affect behavior and personality.
a. Psychoanalytic
b. Trait
c. Cognitive
d. Phenomenological

Answer: c    Page: 3
Topic: Mission Impossible

8.  The task of an employer who compares many job applicants in an attempt to identify one dependable, conscientious, and hard-working individual to hire is similar to that of the _____ psychologist who attempts to identify and assess individual differences.
a. psychoanalytic
b. trait
c. cognitive
d. behavioral

Answer: b    Page: 3
Topic: Mission Impossible

9.  Jeff suspects that his roommate's sexist jokes may indicate he has some hidden, unconscious hos-

tility toward women or that he feels very insecure around women. Jeff's analysis suggests a _____ approach to personality.

a. psychoanalytic
b. trait
c. phenomenological
d. behaviorist

Answer: a    Page: 3
Topic: Mission Impossible

10. Each of the several approaches to personality is good at handling its own key concern

a. but generally ignores the key concerns of the other approaches.
b. as well as the key concerns of the other approaches.
c. and also explains the role of unconscious motivation.
d. and is very effective at changing behavior.

Answer: a    Page: 3
Topic: Mission Impossible

2

# Clues to Personality: The Basic Sources of Data

## *Summary*

All science begins with observation. The observations a scientist makes are called data. For the scientific study of personality, four kinds of data are available, summarized by the acronym LIST. Each kind has advantages and disadvantages. L data comprise observable life outcomes such as being arrested, getting sick, or graduating from college. L data have the advantage of being intrinsically important and of being psychologically relevant at least sometimes, but have the disadvantage of not always being psychologically relevant. I data comprise the judgments of knowledgeable informants about the personality traits of the person being studied. The advantages of I data include the large amount of information on which informants' judgments typically are based, that this information comes from real life, that informants can use common sense, and that the judgments of people who know the person are important because they have a causal force all their own. The disadvantages of I data are that no informant knows everything about another person, that informants' judgments can be biased or subject to errors such as forgetting, and that a few informants may not have common sense. S data comprise the person's own self-judgments of his or her own personality. The advantages of S data are that each individual is the best expert about herself or himself, that S data also have a causal force all their own, and that S data are simple and easy to gather. The disadvantages are that people sometimes will not or cannot tell you about themselves, and that S data may be so easy to obtain that psychologists use them too much. T data comprise direct observations of a person doing something in a testing situation. This situation may be a personality test such as the Rorschach ink blot, a social setting constructed in a psychological labor-atory, or the person's real-life environment. The advantages of T data are that they can look at many different kinds of behaviors, including those that might not occur in normal life, and that because T data are obtained through direct observation they are in a sense objective. The disadvantage of T data is that for all their superficial objectivity, it is still not always clear what they mean, psychologically. Because each kind of data for personality research is potentially valuable *and* potentially misleading, researchers should gather and compare all of them.

## *About the Chapter*

This chapter is about observations. I present a four-part scheme of L data, I data, S data, and T data. Two things are important to note about this scheme. First, it is an adaptation of others with which the instructor might be familiar, such as those by Jack Block and Raymond Cattell. It is not equivalent to those, however. My handling of I data and T data, in particular, are different. Second, many kinds of observations that one can

imagine fall through the cracks of this (and any other) organizational scheme. I don't think this is a fatal flaw; on the contrary, I think it is a worthwhile exercise to put some effort into coming up with ambiguous cases and deciding where they best fit or what they fit between. It helps students to see the range of data that could be relevant for the study of personality.

I have found that the most difficult material to explain in this chapter is my division of personality tests into those that are S data and those that are T data. Indeed, some of my colleagues disagree that this is a useful distinction; an instructor who feels this way should feel free to explain why in lecture. I persist in thinking there is an important difference between true "self-reports" (S data), and questions asked of subjects to gather samples of their behavior rather than find the answer (T data). By this definition, the Self-Monitoring Scale and Stanford Shyness Survey are S data; the MMPI and the Rorschach are T data.

Another unusual aspect of this presentation is that I describe nearly all experiments as gathering T data. That is, they all directly measure some narrow and concrete aspect of a subject's behavior. This categorization means that almost all data gathered by the other subfields of psychology are T data; only personality includes the other three types. It also means that—contrary to claims the students may have heard elsewhere—there is nothing intrinsically superior about direct behavioral observation over other kinds of data because, as the chapter explains, one is never sure about the psychological meaning of T data.

## Teaching Notes

Research methods is a topic that students will perceive right away as forbidding. It is probably not possible to overcome all of their misgivings, but it is worth a try. One possibility is to point out that the question of methods is simply the question, what do you do to find out something else nobody else knows? If you can't look the answer up in a book, what do you do? The answer is "observe the phenomenon" and try to be systematic and organized in how you make your observations, record them, and analyze them. This explanation does not usually make students think methodology is fun, but at least takes it out of the realm of the completely mysterious.

The distinctions between L, I, S, and T data are probably best taught through examples. An instructor could describe some of his or her favorite research studies and ask students what kinds of data are represented. Or, an instructor could ask students to imagine kinds of observations one might make of people, then fit them into the LIST scheme. Some will be ambiguous, and it is probably not a good idea to be overly dogmatic about which classification is "right." The purpose of the LIST scheme is not to infallibly find an unambiguous slot for all possible data, but to illustrate the range of possible data for personality psychology and provide a

vocabulary for how one kind of data is different from another.

## Reader Notes

The two relevant selections for this chapter are the articles in Part I by Craik and by Block. The Craik article is an historical survey of the different methods personality researchers have used over the years. He does not employ the LIST scheme, but a useful exercise for students might be to fit the techniques he describes into this format. The Block article is a specific argument for longitudinal research, which is a topic not emphasized in the text but perhaps worth some mention in lecture. The Block article also mentions the wide range of data his longitudinal project gathers, in terms of his "LOST" scheme which is similar but not exactly equivalent to the LIST scheme I use.

## Discussion Questions

1. *If you wanted to know all about the personality of the person sitting next to you, what would you do?*
2. *Is there anything about a person that, in your opinion, is impossible to know? Is there anything that is unethical to know?*
3. *Can you think of kinds of observations—data—that you could make of a person that would fall outside of the LIST scheme? Which of the four categories comes closest?*

4. *An experimenter gives a subject a long list of math problems that are impossible to solve. The experimenter times how long the subject works on the problems before giving up in disgust. The minutes-and-seconds measure the experimenter has taken is what kind of data? (T data.) The experimenter calls this measure "a real, behavioral measure of persistence." What is right and what is wrong about this label?*

## *Multiple-Choice Questions*

1. There are no perfect _____ of personality, only _____.
   a. measures; devices
   b. indicators; clues
   c. theories; hypotheses
   d. reliable measures; valid measures

   Answer: b    Page: 11
   Topic: Clues to Personality

2. When gathering data or "clues" about personality, the best policy is
   a. gather only a very small number of clues and focus attention on the important ones.
   b. gather only those clues that are certain are not to be misleading.
   c. rely solely on self-report data.
   d. collect as many clues possible.

   Answer: d    Page: 12

Topic: Data Are Clues

3. Easily observable, real life outcomes of possible psychological significance are
   a. S data.
   b. T data.
   c. I data.
   d. L data.

   Answer: d    Page: 13
   Topic: Four Kinds of Clues—L Data

4. Which of the following is an example of L data?
   a. a description of Terry's personality provided by her mother
   b. an observer's count of the number of times Terry laughs during a videotaped laboratory interaction
   c. the number of times Terry has been hospitalized
   d. Terry's response of "true" to the questionnaire item "I enjoy interacting with other people"

   Answer: c    Page: 13
   Topic: Four Kinds of Clues—L Data

5. The primary disadvantage of using L data is that
   a. they may be affected by too many things to tell us much about a person.
   b. they are descriptions based on hundreds of behaviors in many situations.

c. informants may be biased about the person they are judging.

d. all of the above

Answer: a    Page: 14
Topic: Four Kinds of Clues—L Data

6. A major disadvantage of L data is
   a. that they provide a large amount of information.
   b. that informants may only have access to a narrow range of the target's behavior.
   c. their multi-determination.
   d. that judges may be biased about the person they are describing.

Answer: d    Page: 14
Topic: Four Kinds of Clues—L Data

7. I data are
   a. self-judgments.
   b. judgments made by knowledgeable observers.
   c. easily observable, real life outcomes.
   d. direct observations of the subject in some predefined context.

Answer: b    Page: 15
Topic: Four Kinds of Clues—I Data

8. Which of the following is *not* an advantage of I data?
   a. They have causal force.
   b. They include common sense.

c. They are based on large amounts of information.

d. They come from carefully controlled experimental situations.

Answer: d    Page: 15
Topic: Four Kinds of Clues—I Data

9. A personality description of a client by his or her therapist is an example of
   a. S data.
   b. L data.
   c. I data.
   d. T data.

Answer: c    Page: 15
Topic: Four Kinds of Clues—I Data

10. The husband of a participant in a personality research study serves as an informant and provides researchers with a description of the participant's personality. The accuracy of his description is suspect because
   a. it may be biased by his relationship with the participant.
   b. it is based on very brief observations of the participant's behavior in only a few situations.
   c. informants' judgments generally do not include common sense.
   d. all of the above

Answer: a    Page: 16
Topic: Four Kinds of Clues—I Data

11. Different informants may not agree about the personality of a common target individual because
    a. each judge may only see the target person in a limited number of social contexts.
    b. judges may form a mistaken impression based on the recollection of a single, uncharacteristic behavior.
    c. some informants may have biases that affect the accuracy of their judgments.
    d. all of the above

    Answer: d  Pages: 16–21
    Topic: Four Kinds of Clues—I
    Data

12. The judgments of your personality that others form affect your opportunities and expectancies and, as a result, are said to have
    a. generalizability.
    b. validity.
    c. causal force.
    d. reliability.

    Answer: c  Page: 17
    Topic: Four Kinds of Clues—I
    Data

13. In layperson's terms, I data essentially reflect
    a. your internal states or emotions.
    b. your level of self-awareness.
    c. your reputation.
    d. industry data collected in the workplace.

    Answer: c  Page: 17

Topic: Four Kinds of Clues—I
Data

14. Because Jesse's teacher believes that he is intelligent she challenges him with extra assignments and generally encourages his curiosity. At the end of the school year, Jesse performs better on the school's achievement test than any of the other students. Jesse's enhanced performance was likely due to the
    a. recency effect.
    b. expectancy effect.
    c. self-serving bias.
    d. judgment bias.

    Answer: b  Page: 18
    Topic: Four Kinds of Clues—I
    Data

15. The tendency for us to become what other people believe us to be is called the
    a. recency effect.
    b. expectancy effect.
    c. self-serving bias.
    d. judgment bias.

    Answer: b  Page: 18
    Topic: Four Kinds of Clues—I
    Data

16. While completing the NEO Personality Inventory, you answer "true" to the item "I consider myself a nervous person." Your response to this item would be an example of
    a. L data.
    b. I data.
    c. S data.
    d. T data.

Answer: c    Page: 21
Topic: Four Kinds of Clues—S
Data

17. The principle behind S data is
that
a. only a trained personality psychologist can interpret S data.
b. the best information about
personality is obtainable from
real life social outcomes.
c. to assess personality, you
must observe what the person
actually does.
d. you are the world's best expert
about your own personality.

Answer: d    Page: 21
Topic: Four Kinds of Clues—S
Data

18. In order to examine the relationship between early life experiences and adult criminality, Dr.
Robbins asks his research participants to fill out questionnaires
describing their early life. He
then obtains access to copies of
their arrest records from the
county courthouse. The questionnaires used in Dr. Robbins'
study would be _____
while the arrest records would be
_____.
a. L data; T data
b. S data; I data
c. S data; L data
d. T data; L data

Answer: c    Pages: 13, 21
Topic: Four Kinds of Clues

19. _____ are the most frequently used basis for personality
assessment.
a. T data
b. L data
c. S data
d. I data

Answer: c    Page: 22
Topic: Four Kinds of Clues—S
Data

20. Which type of data would most
likely yield the best (i.e., most
accurate) information about the
content of dreams?
a. S data
b. T data
c. L data
d. I data

Answer: a    Page: 23
Topic: Four Kinds of Clues—S
Data

21. Dr. Garcia is attempting to determine what emotions people
are experiencing when they are
fantasizing or daydreaming. To
obtain the most accurate information, Dr. Garcia should use
a. L data
b. I data
c. S data
d. T data

Answer: c    Page: 23
Topic: Four Kinds of Clues—S
Data

22. To obtain S data, a psychologist must
    a. look up information in public records.
    b. recruit informants.
    c. observe the subject directly.
    d. write up a questionnaire.

    Answer: d   Page: 23
    Topic: Four Kinds of Clues—S Data

23. _____ are the most cost-effective data.
    a. S data.
    b. L data.
    c. I data.
    d. T data.

    Answer: a   Page: 23
    Topic: Four Kinds of Clues—S Data

24. Data that derive from the researcher's direct observation of what the subject does in some predefined context are
    a. L data.
    b. I data.
    c. S data.
    d. T data.

    Answer: d   Page: 26
    Topic: Four Kinds of Clues—T Data

25. Beeper and diary reports can be considered compromise
    a. L data.
    b. I data.
    c. S data.
    d. T data.

Answer: d   Pages: 26-27
Topic: Four Kinds of Clues—T Data

26. Which of the following would be an example of natural T data?
    a. reports of the number of times a subject told a joke in a day
    b. the number of seconds a subject waits before seeking help during an experimental emergency situation
    c. a subject's verbal responses to the Rorschach
    d. the number of times a subject interrupts others during a videotaped laboratory situation

    Answer: a   Page: 27
    Topic: Four Kinds of Clues—T Data

27. Asking your co-workers how many times you have stolen a pencil or pen from your employer is an example of
    a. L data.
    b. S data.
    c. I data.
    d. T data.

    Answer: d   Page: 27
    Topic: Four Kinds of Clues—T Data

28. The Thematic Apperception Test and the Rorschach are examples of
    a. L data.
    b. I data.
    c. S data.
    d. T data.

Answer: d    Page: 28
Topic: Four Kinds of Clues—T
Data

29. If, on a personality test, a psychologist asks you a question because he or she wants to know
the answer, the test constitutes
a. S data.
b. L data.
c. I data.
d. T data.

Answer: a    Page: 29
Topic: Four Kinds of Clues—T
Data

30. If, on a personality test, a psychologist asks you a question because he or she wants to see how
you will respond to that stimulus,
the test constitutes
a. S data.
b. I data.
c. L data.
d. T data.

Answer: d    Page: 29
Topic: Four Kinds of Clues—T
Data

# Personality Psychology as Science: Research Methods

## Summary

Psychology puts a great deal of emphasis on the methods by which knowledge can be obtained and in general is more concerned with improving our understanding of human nature than with practical applications. Personality psychology particularly emphasizes the reliability, validity, and generalizability of the measurements that it gathers. Reliability refers to the stability or repeatability of measurements. Validity refers to the degree to which a meas-

**15**

urement actually measures what it is trying to measure. Generalizability is a broader concept that subsumes both reliability and validity, and refers to the class of other measurements to which a given measurement is related. "Representative design" is a technique to maximize the generalizability of one's research results. Psychological data are gathered through experimental and correlational designs. Experimental designs manipulate the variable of interest, whereas correlational designs measure a variable as it already exists in the subjects being studied. Both approaches have advantages and disadvantages. The best way to summarize research results is in terms of effect size, which describes numerically the degree to which one variable is related to another. One good measure of effect size is the correlation coefficient, which can be evaluated with the Binomial Effect Size Display. Ethical issues relevant to psychology include the way research results are used, truthfulness in science, and the use of deception in research with human participants.

## About the Chapter

This chapter covers a lot of ground. Its treatment of reliability, validity, and generalizability is fairly conventional. Not all texts introduce generalizability but I find it useful to do so because that leads naturally to a discussion of facets of generalizability including subjects, stimuli, and responses. The Brunswikian notion of *representative design* is intro-

duced. I believe that to this day Brunswik's fundamental methodological insights are underappreciated and underutilized in psychology.

My treatment of representative design is just the beginning of several aspects of the presentation that could be considered controversial. For example, I compare and contrast correlational and experimental designs. Rather than reach the conventional conclusion (that some students will already have been taught) that experimental designs are intrinsically superior, I note that both designs have advantages and disadvantages that make them equally useful.

Although I explain what it is, I take a stand against significance testing. The statistical literature seems to be evolving rapidly toward a widespread recognition of the point that Paul Meehl made many years ago: Significance levels tell you little if anything, and are often misleading. This message will probably not align with what students have been taught in their statistics classes. An instructor could handle this by noting that the topic is one of current debate and not yet finally resolved, or the instructor could take a stand and either support or argue with my position.

Instead of significance testing, I argue the importance of effect size. The correlation coefficient—my favorite measure of effect size—is briefly explained. I then argue that squaring correlations to yield "variance explained" is an inappropriate practice. As this practice is one that most students are still taught in introductory statistics classes, this surprising message should probably be handled the same way as the one concerning significance testing: State it is a matter of current controversy (it is) and agree or disagree.

The book takes a fair amount of space explaining the use of Rosenthal and Rubin's Binomial Effect Size Display. A surprising number of psychologists don't know about this. While visiting a prominent university to present a colloquium, I once drew a blank 2 x 2 table (like Table 3.1) on the board, added the marginal frequencies and asked the assembled faculty to guess what number went in the upper left-hand corner for a correlation of .30. The first answer, from a methodological expert, was "52?" (the answer is 65). This kind of distorted estimation is what comes of squaring correlation coefficients and underappreciating their size!

It is hard to read much personality research and not see correlation coefficients everywhere. It is important to understand correctly what kinds of effects are being described. That is why I teach the BESD in my course and in the text.

The chapter concludes with a discussion of ethics. The controversial position I take there is quite a hard line against deception in psychological research. I know this a minority position among psychologists, and I urge instructors who disagree with me (as well as those who agree) to present the argument to their students. The main thing is to get students to think about this issue; it matters less what they actually conclude as long as their conclusion is well-reasoned.

## Teaching Notes

I have already mentioned the several controversial positions taken in this chapter and the ways an instructor might want to handle them.

A classroom demonstration of aggregation, akin to the one with meter sticks described in the text, might be useful.

Finally, I suggest the instructor take a class session and talk about correlation coefficients, how they are calculated, and what they mean. This is such a fundamental number for personality research that it is hard to read much literature at all without understanding what it means. Yet, in my experience, most students come out of their statistics classes with only the fuzziest notion of what a correlation is. Typically so much emphasis was put into computational techniques that little conceptual explanation was proffered. Here is an opportunity to remedy that.

## Reader Notes

Several selections in Part II of the Reader tie directly to material in this chapter.

The excerpt by Horowitz (from his statistics book) is a wonderfully clear exposition of the correlation coefficient, and would make a useful backstop to the lecture suggested above. The Reader also includes one of Rosenthal and Rubin's original expositions of the BESD.

Cronbach and Meehl's exposition of construct validity, referred to in the text, is included in the Reader. The other classic article in the methodology of personality is the Campbell-Fiske article, also included. Although we edited both articles down to their bare essentials, students will find them difficult reading. They are included because Cronbach-Meehl and Campbell-Fiske are probably the two most central, classic methodological articles in personality psychology. I sometimes tell students they don't need to read these articles, just to touch them. By this I mean that I want them to have the first-hand experience of seeing the style and content of these important articles, which they will see referred to often throughout the personality literature. It is not particularly important that they understand and absorb every subtle point at this time. I do not discuss the multi-trait multi-method matrix in the text, but this topic and the issues of discriminant and convergent validation might be useful to cover in lecture.

Finally, the Reader presents an excerpt from Abelson's new book that I think is part of the new wave of data analytic thinking. Abelson moves beyond significance testing as the touchstone of statistics and presents a broader view of the use of data analysis for scientific understanding.

## Discussion Questions

1. *In what ways is the psychology of today's college students different from that of your parents? Do you think differently than they do? Would the conclusions of research done with college students also apply to their parents? Can you think of any particular areas where these conclusions would be most likely to be different?*

2. *Will research done on college students also be relevant to members of ethnic minorities, or people who live in other cultures? In what areas would you expect to find the most differences?*

3. *(Students who have taken statistics only): What does a significance level tell you? What does it omit? If we don't use significance to decide if our results mean anything, what can we use instead?*

4. *Is deception in psychological research justified? Does it depend on the research question? Does it depend on the specific kind of deception? Who, if anybody, is harmed by the use of deception in research?*

5. *(Careful with this one): Some psychologists do research on differences between races in intelligence. Let's say members of one race really do have higher IQ scores than members of another. Should we do research to find this out? Or is this issue better left alone? Once the research is done, what would such a result mean? How would it be used?*

6. *Same question as #6, but substitute "gender" for "race."*

## Multiple-Choice Questions

1. According to the text, scientific education is intended to:

a. teach what is known and how to find out what is not yet known.
b. convey what is known about a subject so it can be applied.
c. train individuals in the manufacture of machines and tools.
d. all of the above

Answer: a    Page: 35
Topic: Scientific Education and Technical Training

2.  A _____ would receive technical training while a _____ would receive scientific education.
a. pharmacologist; pharmacist
b. physician; biologist
c. computer scientist; botanist
d. research psychologist; clinical psychologist

Answer: b    Page: 36
Topic: Scientific Education and Technical Training

3.  The effects of irrelevant influences that might tend to lessen your ability to see the trait or state you are trying to measure are called
a. measurement error.
b. confounding variables.
c. aggregating variables.
d. psychometrics.

Answer: a    Page: 36
Topic: Quality of Data—
        Reliability

4.  If you can get the same measurement repeatedly, then your measurement is
a. reliable.
b. valid.
c. significant.
d. generalizable.

Answer: a    Page: 37
Topic: Quality of Data—
        Reliability

5.  A method or instrument that provides the same comparative information repeatedly is
a. valid.
b. reliable.
c. significant.
d. generalizable.

Answer: b    Page: 37
Topic: Quality of Data—
        Reliability

6.  One can increase the reliability of a personality test by
a. aggregating.
b. measuring something important.
c. being careful and using uniform procedures.
d. all of the above

Answer: d    Pages: 37–38
Topic: Quality of Data—
        Reliability

7.  The most important and generally useful way to enhance reliability is
a. to minimize error variance.
b. to measure something that is important.
c. to aggregate your measurements.

d. to maximize error variance.

Answer: c    Page: 37
Topic: Quality of Data—
Reliability

8.  On Friday, Terence completes the Self-Monitoring Scale and receives a score of 49. On the following Tuesday, he fills out the scale again and receives a score of 28. Terence's scores on the Self-Monitoring Scale do not appear to be
    a. valid.
    b. reliable.
    c. significant.
    d. generalizable.

Answer: b    Page: 37
Topic: Quality of Data—
Reliability

9.  Validity is the degree to which a measurement
    a. is consistent and stable.
    b. if repeated, provides the same result.
    c. actually reflects or measures what you think it does.
    d. is reliable.

Answer: c    Page: 39
Topic: Quality of Data—
Validity

10. Jane recently completed the ACME Intelligence Test, a new test that is designed to measure her IQ. She took the test twice and each time received an IQ score of 130, which the test administrator told her indicates that

she is extremely intelligent. However, when Jane completed the Stanford-Binet and the WAIS (two well-established intelligence tests) last month, she scored in the low 70s, indicating that she has an IQ that is well below average. It appears that the ACME Intelligence Scale may be
a. a valid measure of intelligence.
b. a valid but unreliable measure of intelligence.
c. a reliable but not valid measure of intelligence.
d. a more accurate measure of intelligence than the Stanford-Binet or the WAIS.

Answer: c    Page: 39
Topic: Quality of Data—
Validity

11. Reliability is _____ condition for validity.
    a. a necessary and sufficient
    b. a necessary but not sufficient
    c. an unnecessary but sufficient
    d. None of the above. Reliability is irrelevant to the establishment of validity.

Answer: b    Page: 39
Topic: Quality of Data—
Validity

12. A research strategy that involves gathering as many different measurements as you can of a construct and determining if they are correlated is called
    a. construct validation.
    b. aggregation.
    c. generalization.

d. internal validation.

Answer: a    Pages: 39–40
Topic: Quality of Data—
  Validity

13. Reliability and validity are both aspects of a broader concept called
    a. aggregation.
    b. experimental differentiation.
    c. construct validity.
    d. generalizability.

Answer: d    Page: 40
Topic: Quality of Data—
  Generalizability

14. Many researchers, for purposes of convenience, study the behavior of college students and then assume that what they learn applies to people in general. This practice severely limits the
    a. ecological reliability of their research.
    b. internal validity of their studies.
    c. generalizability over subjects.
    d. both a and b

Answer: c    Page: 41
Topic: Quality of Data—
  Generalizability

15. Which of the following sampling methods affords a researcher the greatest generalizability?
    a. randomly selecting introductory psychology students to participate

    b. randomly selecting both high school and college students to participate
    c. recruiting all the executives at a large Fortune 500 company to participate
    d. using a random telephone number dial system to select study participants

Answer: d    Pages: 41–42
Topic: Quality of Data—
  Generalizability

16. The tendency of a group of people who lived at a particular time to be different in some way from those who lived earlier or later is called by psychologists
    a. a generational disparity.
    b. a cohort effect.
    c. the generation gap.
    d. age diversity.

Answer: b    Page: 42
Topic: Quality of Data—
  Generalizability

17. Dr. Jones measures aggression by counting the number of times a research participant hits an inflatable "Bobo doll." If this is the only way Dr. Jones measures aggression, the results of his study may lack
    a. stimulus reliability.
    b. generalizability over responses
    c. predictive validity.
    d. domain specificity.

Answer: b    Page: 42
Topic: Quality of Data—
  Generalizability

18. Egon Brunswik's concept that research should be designed to sample across all of the domains to which the investigator will wish to apply the results is referred to as
   a. generalizability over subjects.
   b. representative design.
   c. ecological reliability.
   d. domain sampling.

   Answer: b   Pages: 43–44
   Topic: Quality of Data—
      Generalizability

19. Dr. Leslie is interested in studying the relationship between mood and willingness to help a stranger. She randomly assigns half of her subjects to the "good mood group" and shows them funny film clips to induce a good mood. The other half of her subjects are assigned to the "bad mood group" and watch boring and unpleasant film clips to induce a bad mood. She then gives every subject an opportunity to donate money to a homeless stranger and measures the amount of money they donate. Dr. Leslie is using
   a. an experimental design.
   b. a correlational design.
   c. a case study design.
   d. a repeated measures design.

   Answer: a   Page: 45
   Topic: Correlational and Experimental Designs

20. Dr. Leslie is interested in studying the relationship between mood and willingness to help a stranger. Every participant in her study completes a mood rating questionnaire, describing his or her current mood. She then gives every subject an opportunity to donate money to a homeless stranger and measures the amount of money he or she donates. Dr. Leslie is using
   a. an experimental design.
   b. a correlational design.
   c. a case study design.
   d. a repeated measures design.

   Answer: b   Page: 45
   Topic: Correlational and Experimental Designs

21. A disadvantage of the experimental method is
   a. that it can create levels of a variable that are unlikely or impossible in real life.
   b. it often requires the use of deception.
   c. the researcher can never be sure what he or she is manipulating and where the causality is actually located.
   d. all of the above

   Answer: d   Pages: 45–46
   Topic: Correlational and Experimental Designs

22. According to the text, the only difference between the experimental and correlational methods is that in the experimental method the presumably causal variable is _____ whereas in the correlational method the same variable is

   _____.

a. externally derived; internally derived
b. significant; important
c. manipulated; measured
d. reliable; valid

Answer: c   Page: 45
Topic: Correlational and Experimental Designs

23. The most touted advantage of the experimental method is
a. that it allows the assessment of causality.
b. that it allows the study of naturally occurring individual differences that already exist in the participants.
c. subjects are always randomly sampled from the general population.
d. all of the above

Answer: a   Page: 45
Topic: Correlational and Experimental Designs

24. If a psychologist describes a research result as "significant," it means that
a. the result is important.
b. the effect is large and dramatic.
c. the result was unlikely to have occurred by chance.
d. the result will likely revolutionize the field.

Answer: c   Page: 47
Topic: Correlational and Experimental Designs

25. A number between −1 and +1 that indexes the association between any two variables is called
a. a significance level.
b. the probability value.
c. the variation index.
d. a correlation coefficient.

Answer: d   Page: 48
Topic: Correlational and Experimental Designs

26. If test scores go down as anxiety goes up, then
a. test scores and anxiety are positively correlated.
b. test scores and anxiety are negatively correlated.
c. test scores and anxiety are unrelated.
d. the correlation between test scores and anxiety would be +1.0.

Answer: b   Page: 48
Topic: Correlational and Experimental Designs

27. A correlation of +.40 between test scores and anxiety means that anxiety accounts for _____ of the variance but _____ of the variation in test scores.
a. 16 percent; 40 percent
b. 40 percent; 4 percent
c. 4 percent; 16 percent
d. 20 percent; 80 percent

Answer: a   Page: 49
Topic: Correlational and Experimental Designs

28. Using the Binomial Effect Size Display, if there is a correlation of +.30 between drinking (or not drinking) alcohol before driving and the likelihood of having (or avoiding) a car accident, then out of 100 people who drink you would expect _____ of them to have an accident.
    a. 100 percent
    b. 60 percent
    c. 90 percent
    d. 65 percent

    Answer: d    Page: 50
    Topic: Correlational and Experimental Designs

29. Assume you are studying 200 subjects, all of whom are sick. An experimental drug is given to 100 of them; the other 100 are given nothing. If the correlation between taking the drug or not, and living or dying, is +.26, then _____ of those who got the drug would still be alive at the end of the study.
    a. 13 percent
    b. 63 percent
    c. 26 percent
    d. 52 percent

    Answer: b    Page: 50
    Topic: Correlational and Experimental Designs

30. The Binomial Effect Size Display is a method for illustrating

    a. heritabilities
    b. validity coefficients
    c. effect sizes
    d. personality coefficients

    Answer: c    Page: 50
    Topic: Correlational and Experimental Designs

**4**

# Personality Traits and Behavior

## *Summary*

The trait approach to personality begins by assuming that individuals differ in their characteristic patterns of thought, feeling, and behavior. These patterns are called personality traits. Classifying people in this way raises an important problem, however: people are inconsistent. Indeed, it has been suggested by some psychologists that people are so inconsistent in their behavior from one situation to the next that it is not worthwhile to try to characterize them in terms of personality traits. The debate among psychologists over this issue was called the consistency controversy. Opponents of traits argue that a review of the personality literature reveals that the ability of traits to predict behavior is extremely limited; that situations are therefore more important than personality traits for determining what people do; and that not only is personality assessment (the measurement of traits) a waste of time, but many of our intuitions about each other are fundamentally wrong. The responses to the first of these arguments are that a fair review of the literature reveals that the predictability of behavior from traits is better than is sometimes acknowledged; that better research methods can make this predictability even higher; and that the upper limit for predictability (a correlation of about .40) is bigger than sometimes recognized. The response to the second of these arguments is that many important effects of situations on behavior are no bigger, statistically, than the documented size of the effects of personality traits on behavior. If the responses to the first two criticisms are valid, then the third, that assessment and our intuitions are both fundamentally flawed, falls apart of its own weight. The many personality trait terms in our language give support to the importance of traits, which provide a useful way to predict behavior and understand personality.

## About the Chapter

A fundamental first issue for personality psychology is, does personality even exist? This is an important issue quite aside from the consistency controversy that occupied the attention of many personality psychologists for about two decades (1968–88). This chapter reviews the consistency controversy and the arguments on both sides.

I was one of the protagonists in this controversy, on the pro-trait side, so it should not be surprising that this chapter basically concludes that Mischel and his critique of personality were mistaken. However, I also explain that the criticism was good for the field because it forced personality psychologists to rethink some of the basic assumptions of personality psychology.

## Teaching Notes

The trick in teaching this material is not to turn off the students by making the consistency controversy seem like the typical academic tempest in a teapot. It is important to avoid the "he said/did not say" tone apparent in

so much of the professional literature when the debate got bogged down in a close reading of comments that Mischel would or would not acknowledge having made. Rather, the focus needs to be kept on the broader issue, which is: in what sense do consistent personality traits really exist? This is a question that is interesting and important regardless of what Mischelians and anti-Mischelians do or do not believe about it, and would be interesting and important even if Mischel had never written his famous critique.

Ever since I first taught the personality course I have regularly included lectures on the person-situation debate. For the first several years I did three lectures, then two, then one. Recently, for the first time, I have omitted this topic from my lectures even though I have included it in the text. Perhaps the controversy really is over, and in a short personality course where choices must be made (I teach on the ten-week quarter system) this is one topic an instructor could safely skip over. On the other hand, the basic issue remains important and many of the substantive and methodological issues raised by the controversy can be helpful in framing discussions of topics that arise later in the course.

## Reader Notes

Three selections in Part II of the Reader are directly relevant to this chapter: the excerpt from Mischel's famous book, the brief rebuttal by Block, and the historical overview of the controversy by Kenrick and Funder.

## Discussion Questions

1. *What are the most consistent aspects of the personalities of the people you know? What are the most inconsistent aspects?*
2. *Do you use personality traits when describing yourself or other people? Are you fooling yourself when you do so?*
3. *Have you ever had somebody else misunderstand your personality by thinking your behavior is more consistent than it really is?*
4. *Next time you talk with your parents explain the consistency issue to them and ask them if they think people have consistent personality traits. Then do the same with college friends who have not taken this course. Are their answers different? How?*

## Multiple-Choice Questions

1. An ultimate criterion for any measurement of a personality trait is whether
   a. it makes the trait easy to understand.
   b. it can be used to predict behavior.
   c. it can be used to measure gender differences.
   d. it is based on ordinary language.

   Answer: b   Page: 59

Topic: Personality Traits and Behavior

2. The trait approach focuses exclusively on
   a. the measurement of absolute levels of traits.
   b. traits that all people have in common.
   c. unique aspects of each individual.
   d. comparative individual differences.

   Answer: d   Page: 60
   Topic: Personality Traits and Behavior

3. One criticism of the trait approach is that it
   a. ignores the trait terms of everyday language.
   b. does not focus on individual differences.
   c. ignores what all people have in common.
   d. denies that situations have any affect on behavior.

   Answer: c   Page: 60
   Topic: The Measurement of Individual Differences

4. The trait approach is based on empirical research
   a. that is mostly correlational in nature.
   b. that is mostly experimental in nature.
   c. from case studies.
   d. from archival studies.

   Answer: a   Page: 60

Topic: The Measurement of Individual Differences

5. According to Kluckhohn and Murray, "Every man is in certain respects (a) like all other men, (b) like some other men, (c) like no other man." Which section of this quote most closely reflects what trait psychologists study?
   a. like all other men
   b. like some other men
   c. like no other man
   d. all of the above

Answer: b    Page: 60
Topic: The Measurement of Individual Differences

6. A fundamental problem for the trait approach is that
   a. individual differences cannot be measured reliably.
   b. situations do not affect behavior.
   c. people are inconsistent.
   d. correlational methods do not provide ready indices of effect size.

Answer: c    Page: 61
Topic: People Are Inconsistent

7. Walter Mischel and his 1968 book, *Personality and Assessment*, are of historical importance because Mischel
   a. provided the most cogent argument for why trait theory and psychodynamic theory should be integrated.
   b. is credited with starting the person-situation debate by claiming that personality is an unimportant factor in behavioral prediction.
   c. provided the first real defense of trait theory against the situationist attack.
   d. is the first modern researcher to begin to scientifically validate some of Freud's claims about the unconscious.

Answer: b    Page: 63
Topic: The Person-Situation Debate

8. In his book, *Personality and Assessment*, Walter Mischel argued that
   a. traits are the only factors that influence human behavior.
   b. situations do not reliably predict consistent behavioral trends.
   c. behavior is too inconsistent to allow individual differences to be characterized in terms of broad personality traits.
   d. personality traits transcend the immediate situation and moment and provide the most consistent guide to a person's actions.

Answer: c    Page: 63
Topic: The Person-Situation Debate

9. The situationist argument, as presented in Mischel's *Personality and Assessment*, holds that
   a. a thorough review of the literature reveals that there is a limit to how well one can predict behavior from personality.

b. situations are more important than personality traits for determining behavior.

c. our everyday intuitions about people are fundamentally flawed.

d. all of the above

Answer: d   Page: 64
Topic: The Person-Situation
Debate

10. Walter Mischel, in his book *Personality and Assessment*, argued that behavior is best predicted from
a. situations.
b. personality variables.
c. motivations.
d. goals.

Answer: a   Page: 64
Topic: The Person-Situation
Debate

11. Situationism is the position that
a. situations do not influence behavior.
b. situations are more important than personality traits in determining behavior.
c. the ability of personality traits to predict behavior is severely limited.
d. both b and c

Answer: d   Page: 64
Topic: The Person-Situation
Debate

12. The behavioral measurements used in the studies reviewed by Mischel were

a. most frequently taken from real life settings.
b. nearly all gathered in laboratory settings.
c. garnered from clinicians' case studies.
d. archival data.

Answer: b   Page: 64
Topic: The Person-Situation
Debate

13. A correlation coefficient is a number that ranges between
a. .30 and .40.
b. 1 and 100.
c. −1 and +1.
d. zero and infinity.

Answer: c   Page: 65
Topic: The Person-Situation
Debate

14. If there is a positive correlation between extraversion and risk-taking then
a. the researcher can be certain that extraversion causes risk-taking.
b. the higher a person's extraversion score, the more risks he or she is likely to take.
c. the lower a person's extraversion score, the more risks he or she is likely to take.
d. the researcher can be certain that extraversion and risk-taking are unrelated.

Answer: b   Page: 65
Topic: The Person-Situation
Debate

15. According to situationists, the range of personality coefficients is
    a. .30 to .40.
    b. 1 to 100.
    c. −1 to +1.
    d. zero to infinity.

Answer: a    Page: 65
Topic: The Person-Situation Debate

16. The Mischelian argument is that correlations between personality and behavior, or between behavior in one situation and behavior in another,
    a. are usually between .50 and .60 and are small.
    b. are essentially zero.
    c. are large and important.
    d. seldom exceed .30 or .40.

Answer: d    Page: 65
Topic: The Person-Situation Debate

17. One kind of research improvement offered in response to the situationist critique suggests identifying those individuals whose behavior is more consistent than others. This research improvement involves
    a. aggregating multiple measurements.
    b. using a moderator variable approach.
    c. employing the BESD.
    d. predicting actions at particular moments rather than general behavioral trends.

Answer: b    Page: 67

Topic: The Person-Situation Debate

18. Which of the following behaviors would be the easiest to predict accurately?
    a. Mary will smile at 10:00 tomorrow morning.
    b. At a party on Friday, Susan will talk to at least ten people.
    c. David will generally be on time for work next week.
    d. None of the above. Each of these behaviors would be easy to predict.

Answer: c    Page: 67
Topic: The Person-Situation Debate

19. Which of the following behaviors would tend to be consistent across situations?
    a. speaking loudly
    b. trying to impress someone
    c. dominating another person
    d. cooperating with teammates

Answer: a    Page: 67
Topic: The Person-Situation Debate

20. Which of the following would be an example of using a moderator variable approach to improve the predictability of behavior from personality?
    a. measuring how frequently you are late to work using a daily diary report of your everyday behavior
    b. collecting information about your responses in stressful work situations

c. trying to predict how warm and friendly you will act when you meet your new in-laws next Monday
d. determining if the behavior of high self-monitors is less consistent than that of low self-monitors

Answer: d   Page: 67
Topic:  The Person-Situation Debate

21. In order to improve personality research, researchers can
   a. check for moderator variables.
   b. predict behavioral trends rather than single acts.
   c. measure behavior in real life.
   d. all of the above

Answer: d   Page: 67
Topic:  The Person-Situation Debate

22. One difficulty with the moderator variable approach is that
   a. no potential moderators have yet to be identified by researchers.
   b. many direct behavioral measurements must be taken.
   c. real life behaviors are not easy to assess.
   d. moderator variables are subtle and difficult to measure.

Answer: d   Page: 68
Topic:  The Person-Situation Debate

23. Traditionally, the routine practice to evaluate the degree to which

behavior is affected by the situation has been to
   a. square the correlation coefficient for the relationship between behavior and some aspect of the situation.
   b. determine the percentage of variance accounted for by personality, subtract that from 100 percent, and then assign the remaining percentage of the variance, by default, to the situation.
   c. add the variance in the behavioral measure to the variance for the situational variable.
   d. use the correlation coefficient for the relationship between the behavioral measure and the situational variable an indicator of effect size.

Answer: b   Page: 70
Topic:  The Person-Situation Debate

24. Historically, to evaluate the effects of personality variables, personality psychologists have concentrated on _____.
To evaluate the effects of situational variables, social psychologists have concentrated on

_____.
   a. variance; standard deviations
   b. standard deviations; variance
   c. effect size; statistical significance
   d. statistical significance; effect size

Answer: c   Page: 71
Topic:  The Person-Situation Debate

25. Funder and Ozer (1983) examined the results of three classic social psychological studies. They converted the results to effect sizes and found that the effects were typically equivalent to correlations in the range of

    _____.

    a. .10 to .20
    b. .30 to .40
    c. .61 to .75
    d. .70 to .97
    Answer: b    Pages: 71–72
    Topic: The Person-Situation Debate

26. Funder and Ozer (1983) converted the results of three classic social psychological studies to effect sizes. After comparing those effect sizes with those typically obtained by personality psychologists, Funder and Ozer concluded that
    a. situational variables, like personality variables, cannot predict behavior.
    b. both situational and personality variables are important determinants of behavior.
    c. the upper limit for a situation coefficient is only .20.
    d. the three studies were so fundamentally flawed that they don't allow us to conclude anything about the predictability of behavior from situational variables.

    Answer: b    Page: 73
    Topic: The Person-Situation Debate

27. According to the text, the most plausible explanation for the 17.953 trait terms found by Allport and Odbert (1936) is that
    a. we need ways to describe important psychological differences among people.
    b. their methodology was biased toward finding many terms.
    c. trait terms are essentially redundant because we have many different words for the same small set of traits.
    d. we simply make up differences between the personalities of people know and assign words to describe these perceived differences.

    Answer: a    Pages: 73–74
    Topic: The Person-Situation Debate

28. The upward trend in the number of trait terms in the English language is evidence that
    a. we need them to discriminate between different types of people.
    b. personality traits are an important part of our culture.
    c. when it comes to personality, one sizes does not fit all.
    d. all of the above

    Answer: d    Pages: 73–74
    Topic: The Person-Situation Debate

29. A review of the research on the predictability of behavior from personality traits indicates that

a. behavior can never be reliably predicted from personality variables.
b. the predictability of behavior from personality is better than is sometimes acknowledged.
c. the predictability of behavior from situations is worse than the predictability from personality.
d. Mischel was right.

Answer: b    Page: 75
Topic: The Person-Situation Debate

# Personality Assessment I: Personality Testing and Its Consequences

## *Summary*

Any characteristic pattern of behavior, thought, and emotional experience that exhibits relative consistency across time and situations is part of an individual's personality. These patterns include personality traits as well as such psychological attributes as goals, moods, and strategies. Personality assessment is a frequent activity of industrial and clinical psychologists and researchers. Everybody also performs personality assessments of the people they know in daily life. An important issue for assessments, whether by psychologists or by laypersons, is the degree to which those assessments are correct. This chapter examines how psychologists' personality tests are constructed and validated. Some personality tests comprise S data and others comprise T data, but a more commonly drawn distinction is between projective tests and objective tests. Projective tests try to gain insight into personality by presenting subjects with ambiguous stimuli, and recording how the subjects respond. Objective tests ask subjects specific questions, and assess personality on the basis of how the subjects answer. Objective tests can be constructed by rational, factor analytic, or empirical methods, and the modern practice is to use a combination of all three methods. Some people are uncomfortable with the practice of personality assessment because they see it as an unfair invasion of privacy. However, because people inevitably judge each others' personalities, the real issue is how personality assessment should be done—through informal intuitions or more formalized techniques.

## About the Chapter

Most of this chapter is a straightforward exposition of the methods of constructing and evaluating personality tests. It includes some recent developments, including some legal troubles that users of the Minnesota Multiphasic Personality Inventory (MMPI) have experienced. The chapter concludes with a discussion of the ethics of personality testing.

## Teaching Notes

I have found that students are more interested in this material if illustrations of actual personality tests are employed as often as possible. For example, it is an entertaining and useful exercise to show students Ror

schach ink blots or Thematic Apperception Test (TAT) pictures and have them write their responses. You can have them write their responses anonymously and exchange them randomly, and then try to evaluate the meaning of the responses they are given. Many self-report personality tests can be administered in a classroom setting as well.

My favorite for this purpose is the Self-Monitoring Scale (included later in the text as Table 7.7). Sometimes I have students complete this test before reading any of the material in Chapters 4–7. The nice thing about this scale is that the property it was designed to measure is interesting but non-threatening. Nobody is likely to be traumatized by his or her Self-Monitoring score; nearly everybody seems to get the score they would desire (i.e., high self-monitors *want* to be high self-monitors).

The ethics of personality testing can trigger interesting and useful discussions. First, it is important to remind students not to be swept away by the technology, physical appearance, and interest value of personality tests. They still are of limited validity, and even though many are valid enough to be useful, none are perfect. In particular, I warn my students that if they ever take a personality test that tells them something about themselves they believe to be untrue, the odds are at least 90–10 that they are right and the test is wrong. Students should also be warned about the "Barnum effect"—that people usually find generally-worded personality descriptions of themselves persuasive, even when everybody is given the same description

## Reader Notes

The relevant sections of the reader are the O'Connor and Allport selections in Part II, which define in different ways what trait assessment is all about.

## Discussion Questions

1.  *If you wanted to understand someone's personality and could only ask him or her three questions, what would those questions be? What traits would the answers reveal?*
2.  *How would you choose somebody to be your roommate? your employee? a date? Would personality traits be relevant to your choice? How would you try to evaluate those traits?*
3.  *Have you ever taken a personality test? Did the results seem accurate? Were the results useful?*
4.  *How many uses can you think of for knowing somebody's personality-test score? Are any (or all) of these uses unethical?*

## Multiple-Choice Questions

1.  Personality assessment refers to
    a.  a plan designed to treat personality disorders.
    b.  the analysis and interpretation of genetic markers of personality.
    c.  the measurement of any characteristic pattern of behavior, thought, or emotion.
    d.  the selection of a group individuals with the most unique temperaments.

    Answer: c    Page: 76
    Topic: The Nature of Personality Assessment

2.  When professional personality judgments are evaluated, it is typically said that we are evaluating their
    a.  accuracy.
    b.  validity.
    c.  reliability.
    d.  agreement.

    Answer: b    Page: 77
    Topic: The Nature of Personality Assessment

3.  When amateur personality judgments are evaluated, it is typically said that we are evaluating their
    a.  accuracy.
    b.  validity.
    c.  reliability.
    d.  agreement.

    Answer: a    Page: 77
    Topic: The Nature of Personality Assessment

4.  The two basic criteria for evaluating the validity of a personality judgment are
    a.  rationality and empiricism.
    b.  usefulness and practicality.

c. agreement and behavioral prediction.
d. consensus and ability to generate testable hypotheses.

Answer: c    Page: 77
Topic: The Nature of Personality Assessment

5. The MMPI was designed to:
a. clinically assess individuals with psychological disorders.
b. assess nondisturbed individuals.
c. identify the Big Five personality factors.
d. measure multiple aspects of productivity and ingenuity in workers.

Answer: a    Page: 79
Topic: Personality Tests

6. The California Psychological Inventory was designed to
a. clinically assess individuals with psychological disorders.
b. assess nondisturbed individuals.
c. identify the Big Five personality factors.
d. measure multiple aspects of productivity and ingenuity in workers.

Answer: b    Page: 79
Topic: Personality Tests

7. Your responses to the item "I am an intelligent person" would be _____ data while your score on an intelligence test that reflects the number of prob-

lems you got right would be
_____.
a. T data; L data
b. S data; L data
c. I data; T data
d. S data; T data

Answer: d    Page: 80
Topic: Personality Tests

8. _____ ask a respondent to interpret a meaningless, ambiguous stimulus in order to access the inner workings of the person's mind.
a. Rationally constructed tests
b. Projective tests
c. Factor analytic tests
d. Objective tests

Answer: b    Page: 80
Topic: Personality Tests—Projective Tests

9. All projective tests
a. involve stimuli with no clear meaning.
b. involve the construction of stories and narratives.
c. require choosing among multiple, predetermined alternatives.
d. rely on computer scoring methods.

Answer: a    Page: 80
Topic: Personality Tests—Projective Tests

10. A psychologist adminstering the Thematic Apperception Test (TAT) asks respondents to

a. draw a person so that she may determine which parts are left out or exaggerated.
b. describe their current level of hostility so that she can measure their Type A tendencies.
c. tell stories about pictures she shows them to assess their motivational state.
d. describe their perceptions of the causes of people's behavior so that she can measure attributional complexity.

Answer: c   Page: 81
Topic: Personality Tests—
    Projective Tests

11. Which projective test appears to have evidence that comes close to establishing its validity?
a. the Draw-a-Person Test
b. the Thematic Apperception Test (TAT)
c. the Rorschach Ink Blot Test
d. both b and c

Answer: d   Page: 81
Topic: Personality Tests—
    Projective Tests

12. One problem with projective tests is that
a. two different interpreters of the same response might come to different conclusions about the scoring and meaning of the response.
b. once a cluster of items has been identified as being inter-correlated, a psychologist must decide how the items are conceptually related.

c. although the items discriminate between groups, the content of the items may seem contrary or absurd to test takers.
d. you must identify different criterion groups before you can develop your test.

Answer: a   Page: 81
Topic: Personality Tests—
    Projective Tests

13. If a test consists of a list of true/false questions and is graded using a computer-scorable answer sheet, then it is:
a. a projective test.
b. a Q-sort.
c. an objective test.
d. a commonality scale.

Answer: c   Page: 82
Topic: Personality Tests—
    Objective Tests

14. If everybody read, interpreted, and answered an item in exactly the same way, then that item would
a. not be very useful for the assessment of individual differences.
b. be very informative about personality.
c. have been developed using the rational method of test construction.
d. be empirically derived.

Answer: a   Page: 82
Topic: Personality Tests—
    Objective Tests

15. The commonality scale on the CPI is
    a. used to identify individuals who are deliberately attempting to sabotage a test.
    b. used to detect illiterates who are pretending to know how to read.
    c. a subset of items that are answered in the same way by at least 95 percent of all people.
    d. all of the above

    Answer: d    Page: 83
    Topic: Personality Tests—
    Objective Tests

16. According to Gough, when individuals encounter a commonality item, they
    a. believe the item to be dumb and obvious.
    b. like the item because it is not ambiguous.
    c. lie in order to appear unique.
    d. always answer "true" rather than "false."

    Answer: b    Page: 83
    Topic: Personality Tests—
    Objective Tests

17. Dr. Akita's test, which is designed to measure sociability, contains a set of items that seem directly and obviously related to sociability such as "I like to go to parties" or "I enjoy the company of other people." Which method of test construction is Dr. Akita using?
    a. empirical method
    b. factor analytic method
    c. rational method

d. projective method

Answer: c    Page: 83
Topic: Methods of Objective
Test Construction

18. The basis of the _____ method of test construction is to come up with items that seem directly, obviously, and logically related to what it is you wish to measure.
    a. rational
    b. empirical
    c. philosophical
    d. factor analytic

Answer: a    Page: 83
Topic: Methods of Objective
Test Construction

19. For any rationally constructed personality scale to work, it must satisfy which of the following conditions?
    a. The items on the form must all be valid indicators of what the tester is trying to measure.
    b. The person who completes the form must be willing to accurately report his or her self-assessment.
    c. Each item must mean the same thing to the person who fills out the form as it did to the psychologist who wrote it.
    d. All of the above conditions must be satisfied for the scale to work.

Answer: d    Page: 84
Topic: Methods of Objective
Test Construction

20. Tests developed using
_____ methods of
test construction are currently the
most common form of psychological measurement device.
   a. factor analytic
   b. rational
   c. empirical
   d. a combination of

   Answer: b    Page: 85
   Topic:  Methods of Objective
   Test Construction

21. The factor analytic technique is
designed to
   a. identify individuals who are
      attempting to lie or sabotage a
      test.
   b. identify groups of test items
      that co-occur.
   c. identify items that mean the
      same thing to the respondent
      as they do to the researcher.
   d. analyze and score responses
      to projective tests.

   Answer: b    Page: 86
   Topic:  Methods of Objective
   Test Construction

22. The approach to personality-test
construction that examines a set
of correlations among many variables to identify patterns of co-
variations is called the
_____ approach.
   a. nomothetic
   b. idiographic
   c. rational
   d. factor analytic

   Answer: d    Page: 87

   Topic:  Methods of Objective
   Test Construction

23. Currently, an emerging consensus among personality researchers is that there are
_____ fundamental
traits.
   a. three
   b. five
   c. sixteen
   d. twenty

   Answer: b    Page: 87
   Topic:  Methods of Objective
   Test Construction

24. A limitation of the factor analytic approach is that
   a. sometimes the factors that
      emerge do not make sense.
   b. you cannot use everyday trait
      terms for your scale.
   c. the test is only as good as the
      criterion groups on which it
      was based.
   d. the items that go into the
      analysis must all be empiri-
      cally derived.

   Answer: a    Page: 88
   Topic:  Methods of Objective
   Test Construction

25. The Big Five are:
   a. Freudian psychoanalytic
      stages of personality devel-
      opment.
   b. steps in the construction of
      empirical tests.
   c. factor analytically derived di-
      mensions of personality.

d. the primary methods of test construction used by personality psychologists.

Answer: c    Page: 88
Topic: Methods of Objective Test Construction

26. The sole basis by which items are selected for empirically derived personality scales is whether
   a. their content adequately reflects the construct to be measured.
   b. they are correlated with other items on the scales.
   c. the respondent will be willing and able to truthfully give an accurate self-assessment for them.
   d. they are answered differently by different kinds of people.

Answer: d    Page: 90
Topic: Methods of Objective Test Construction

27. Faking responses in order to influence test results is most difficult on _____ constructed tests.
   a. factor analytically
   b. empirically
   c. rationally
   d. nomothetically

Answer: b    Page: 91
Topic: Methods of Objective Test Construction

28. The Personality Research Form (PRF) developed by Douglas

Jackson was developed using _____ methods.
   a. rational
   b. factor analytic
   c. empirical
   d. a combination of

Answer: d    Page: 93
Topic: Methods of Objective Test Construction

29. Integrity tests administered in pre-employment screening provide good measures of
   a. conscientiousness.
   b. intelligence.
   c. drug use on the job.
   d. sociability.

Answer: a    Page: 94
Topic: Purposes of Personality Testing

30. One objection to the use of vocational interest tests is that these tests
   a. measure conscientiousness rather than vocational interest.
   b. may prevent women or minority group members from joining certain fields.
   c. measure performance ability rather than job interest.
   d. can be used to tell individuals what kind of occupational group they most resemble.

Answer: b    Page: 94
Topic: Purposes of Personality Testing

31. One conclusion that has been made about testing is that eliminating the use of personality tests in employment screening will
    a. prevent biases from affecting hiring decisions.
    b. decrease the likelihood that women and minorities will be discriminated against in hiring.
    c. increase the use of lie-detector tests and drug tests in employment screening.
    d. not prevent traits from being judged but will change how they will be judged.

Answer: d    Page: 95
Topic:  Purposes of Personality Testing

6

# Personality Assessment II: Personality Judgment in Daily Life

## *Summary*

People judge the personalities of each other and of themselves all the time, and these judgments often have important consequences. The judgments of others can affect your opportunities and create self-fulfilling prophecies, or expectancy effects. Your judgments of yourself influence what you are likely to attempt to accomplish in life. Therefore, it is important to examine when and how judgments of the self and of others are accurate. Recent research evaluates the accuracy of personality judgment in terms of agreement and predictive validity. That is, judgments that agree with judgments from other sources (such as other people) or that are able to predict the people judged are deemed more likely to be accurate than judgments that do not agree with each other or that cannot predict behavior. Research has examined four kinds of variables that seem to affect the likelihood of accurate personality judgment: (1) the good judge, or the possibility that some judges are more accurate than others; (2) the good target, or the possibility that some individuals are easier to judge than others; (3) the good trait, or the possibility that some traits are easier to judge accurately than others; and (4) good information, or the possibility that more or better information about the target makes accurate judgment more likely. This research has led recently to a model of the process of accurate personality judgment that describes it as a function of the relevance, availability, detection, and utilization of behavioral cues.

## About the Chapter

The most important point of this chapter is that personality assessment is not something done only by personality psychologists. Everybody does it in daily life. And the very same criteria by which one would evaluate the "validity" of a personality test can and should be applied to evaluating the "accuracy" of a personality judgment. This is the place where personality psychology intersects with social psychology, and therefore this chapter is the most social-psychological one in the text. For those students who have already taken a course in social psychology, it might be useful to remind them of this fact and point out that the material in this chapter could seem familiar, but will be interpreted rather differently than in most social psychology texts. Specifically, I treat lay personality judgments not merely as interesting perceptions, but as assessments that just might be accurate.

## Teaching Notes

It should not be difficult to convey the major point of this chapter, that personality assessment is a ubiquitous feature of daily life. Lectures can include numerous real-life examples, perhaps from the instructor's personal experience. It is also worth impress

ing upon students the idea that the question of accuracy in personality judgment does not have a simple answer. It is not meaningful to say that people are generally accurate or inaccurate; instead we need to find out when people are more and less likely to be accurate. This is the purpose of the four moderators of accuracy discussed in this chapter (judge, target, trait, and information).

For instructors familiar with this background, the similarity between the model in Figure 6.1 and the Brunswik lens model could be developed in more detail. Research on the accuracy of personality judgment is active and the literature is rapidly expanding. An instructor might find it worthwhile to leaf through recent issues of the *Journal of Personality and Social Psychology, Journal of Personality,* and *Journal of Research in Personality* and look for articles by Colvin, Funder, Ickes, Kenny, Jussim, Paulhus, or Swann to bring the latest findings into the classroom.

## Reader Notes

Material on the accuracy of personality judgment—such as my own research—was not included in the Reader for reasons of space and because it is often seen as being part of social psychology as well as or instead of personality psychology. An interested instructor could assign my theoretical article (*Psychological Review*, 1995, *102*, 652-670). The O'Connor selection in Part II of the Reader is a nice illustration of the everyday use of personality traits.

## Discussion Questions

1. When you judge the personality of others are you usually right or wrong?

2. When others judge your personality, are they usually right or wrong? When they are mistaken, why does this happen?

3. Under what circumstances do you find the personality of other people easiest to judge? Does your accuracy depend on the setting in which you meet them, what they are like, what you are like, or how you feel?

4. Under what circumstances do you find the personality of other people hardest to judge? Consider the same moderators as in Question 3.

5. Have you taken a course in social psychology? If so, how was that course's treatment of the topic of person perception similar to and different from the present treatment of personality judgment?

## Multiple-Choice Questions

1. The judgments other people make of your personality may affect your
   a. opportunities.
   b. chances of getting a job.
   c. expectancies.
   d. all of the above

   Answer: d   Page: 99
   Topic: Consequences of Lay
      Judgments of Personality

2. Self-fulfilling prophecies are more technically known as
   a. opportunistic fallacies.
   b. expectancy effects.
   c. consequential reputations.
   d. recency effects.

   Answer: b   Page: 99
   Topic: Consequences of Lay
      Judgments of Personality

3. Chronically shy people
   a. are seldom lonely.
   b. do not want to form friendships.
   c. may not develop normal social skills.
   d. all of the above

   Answer: c   Page: 99
   Topic: Consequences of Lay
      Judgments of Personality

4. Shy people are typically perceived by others to be
   a. shy.
   b. cold and aloof.
   c. warm and friendly.
   d. sensitive and intelligent.

   Answer: b   Page: 99
   Topic: Consequences of Lay
      Judgments of Personality

5. Julie doesn't like to go to parties because she is afraid people won't like her. When she does go, she avoids eye contact, gives short, abrupt responses to other people's questions, and quickly withdraws from all interactions. As a result, she spends most of

the evening in a corner by herself, convinced that no one at the party likes her. This is an example of

a. the causal force of I data.
b. expectancy effects.
c. the effects of low self-monitoring.
d. an internal locus of control.

Answer: b   Page: 99
Topic: Consequences of Lay Judgments of Personality

6. In a series of studies by Rosenthal and Jacobson (1968), the IQ of "late bloomers" increased by an average of about 15 points. These studies demonstrated

a. the power of expectancies.
b. that formal training designed to develop self-efficacy can impact performance.
c. the accuracy of lay judgments of personality.
d. the "good target" moderator of accuracy.

Answer: a   Page: 100
Topic: Consequences of Lay Judgments of Personality

7. In the Snyder, Tanke, & Berscheid (1977) experiment, if the male subject had been shown a photograph of an attractive woman, the female subject

a. rated herself as more attractive than the woman in the photograph.
b. rated herself as less attractive than the woman in the photograph.

c. was rated by other people as behaving in a warm, humorous, and friendly manner.
d. was rated by other people as behaving in a cold, aloof, and unfriendly manner.

Answer: c   Page: 101
Topic: Consequences of Lay Judgments of Personality

8. Attractive females are expected to be warm and friendly, and those thought to be attractive are treated in such a manner that they indeed respond that way. According to Snyder, Tanke, and Berscheid (1977), this effect is a form of

a. self-fulfilling prophecy.
b. accuracy moderator.
c. sex discrimination.
d. the judgability phenomena.

Answer: a   Page: 101
Topic: Consequences of Lay Judgments of Personality

9. According to Lee Jussim (1991), the source of real life expectancies is likely

a. erroneous stereotypes about groups.
b. previous observations of behavioral tendencies.
c. authoritarian personality traits.
d. a cognitive bias to seek incongruent information.

Answer: b   Page: 102
Topic: Consequences of Lay Judgments of Personality

10. The complete assembly of all the judgments you make about your personality and all the opinions you have about yourself is called your
    a. self-monitor.
    b. sense of self-efficacy.
    c. self-concept.
    d. self-consciousness.

    Answer: c    Page: 103
    Topic: Consequences of Lay
        Judgments of Personality

11. People who believe that the important forces within their lives come from within themselves and think that they can affect what happens to them
    a. have an external locus of control.
    b. have an internal locus of control.
    c. tend to be high self-monitors.
    d. tend to low self-monitors.

    Answer: b    Page: 104
    Topic: Consequences of Lay
        Judgments of Personality

12. Jeanine believes that no matter what she does, she won't have the wedding she's always dreamed about. Her mother will choose the bridal gown, caterer, and florist and she won't be able to do a thing about it. Jeanine most likely has
    a. high self-esteem.
    b. an internal locus of control.
    c. a tendency to self-monitor.
    d. an external locus of control.

    Answer: d    Page: 104

Topic: Consequences of Lay
    Judgments of Personality

13. _____
    refers to your beliefs about what you will and will not be able to accomplish.
    a. Self-efficacy
    b. Self-esteem
    c. Self-consciousness
    d. Self-generativity

    Answer: a    Page. 104
    Topic: Consequences of Lay
        Judgments of Personality

14. The basic reason research on accuracy experienced a lengthy hiatus between 1955 and the mid-1980s wasthat
    a. early researchers had already identified the characteristics of the "good judge" of personality.
    b. researchers turned their attention to studying the content of personality judgments.
    c. researchers lacked a consensual criteria for determining the accuracy of a personality judgment.
    d. early research indicated that personality judgments are relatively inconsequential.

    Answer: c    Page: 105
    Topic: The Accuracy of Lay
        Judgments of Personality

15. "There is no such thing as objective reality, only human ideas or perceptions of reality." This statement would most likely be made by

a. a constructivist.
b. a critical realist.
c. a social perceptualist.
d. a judgmentalist.

Answer: a   Page: 105
Topic: The Accuracy of Lay
    Judgments of Personality

16. "The absence of perfect, infalli-
    ble criteria for truth does not
    force us to conclude that all in-
    terpretations of reality are
    equally likely to be correct."
    This statement would most likely
    be made by
    a. a constructivist.
    b. a critical realist.
    c. a social perceptualist.
    d. a judgmentalist.

Answer: b   Page: 105
Topic: The Accuracy of Lay
    Judgments of Personality

17. The observation that if it looks
    like a duck, walks like a duck,
    and quacks like a duck then it is
    probably a duck refers to the
    method of
    a. reliability moderation.
    b. boundary establishment.
    c. procedural judgment.
    d. convergent validation.

Answer: d   Page: 106
Topic: The Accuracy of Lay
    Judgments of Personality

18. Which of the following illustrates
    converging criteria that could be
    used to establish the accuracy of
    a personality judgment?

a. Your friends describe you as
   an extravert.
b. You always show up to work
   on time and your colleagues
   say that you are dependable
   and conscientious.
c. You tend to experience extreme emotions and throw
   tantrums frequently.
d. You describe yourself as intelligent but you get a low
   score on an IQ test.

Answer: b   Page: 106
Topic: The Accuracy of Lay
    Judgments of Personality

19. One difficulty early researchers
    encountered in identifying the
    "good judge" of personality was
    that
    a. a good judge in one context
       was not always a good judge
       in other contexts.
    b. clinical psychologists dis-
       missed the findings, claiming
       good judgment of others re-
       quired extensive training.
    c. the identified traits were not
       clearly a functional part of a
       specific ability to judge peo-
       ple.
    d. both a and c

Answer: d   Page: 107
Topic: The Accuracy of Lay
    Judgments of Personality

20. Early research on the "good
    judge" of personality indicated
    that the "good judge" was
    a. extraverted.
    b. a high self-monitor.
    c. narcissistic.

d. intelligent.

Answer: d   Page: 107
Topic: The Accuracy of Lay
   Judgments of Personality

21. Recent research by John and
    Robins (1994) indicates that
    _____ and _____
    tend to be poor judges of per-
    sonality.
    a. extraverts; depressives
    b. introverts; highly intelligent
       individuals
    c. narcissists; self-diminishers
    d. authoritarian personalities;
       high self-monitors

Answer: c   Page: 107
Topic: The Accuracy of Lay
   Judgments of Personality

22. Kolar, Funder, and Colvin com-
    pared the judgmental ability of
    the self and acquaintances using
    behavioral prediction as their
    criterion. Their results indicated
    that
    a. the self judgments consistently
       had better predictive validity
       than the acquaintance judg-
       ments.
    b. acquaintance judgments con-
       sistently had better predictive
       validity than self judgments.
    c. there was no difference in the
       predictive validity of self and
       acquaintance judgments on
       any measures.
    d. the self judgments had better
       predictive validity but only
       for visible traits.

Answer: b   Page: 107-108

Topic: The Accuracy of Lay
   Judgments of Personality

23. Robert is a stable, well-adjusted
    person. His behavior is fairly
    consistent and predictable. Es-
    sentially, with Robert, "what you
    see is what you get." Robert
    would most likely be
    a. easy to judge accurately.
    b. a good judge of personality.
    c. a narcissist.
    d. a self-diminisher.

Answer: a   Pages: 109–10
Topic: The Accuracy of Lay
   Judgments of Personality

24. Which of the following traits
    would be easiest to judge accu-
    rately?
    a. moodiness
    b. talkativeness
    c. ruminativeness
    d. all of the above

Answer: b   Page: 110
Topic: The Accuracy of Lay
   Judgments of Personality

25. Which of the following would
    moderate the ability to judge a
    specific trait?
    a. judgability
    b. unpredictability
    c. visibility
    d. acquaintanceship

Answer: c   Page: 110
Topic: The Accuracy of Lay
   Judgments of Personality

26. Finding that more-observable traits yield better interjudge agreement strongly suggests that peer judgment is based on
    a. a manufactured reputation.
    b. the target's self-judgments.
    c. direct behavioral observation.
    d. stereotypes.

    Answer: c    Page: 111
    Topic: The Accuracy of Lay
    Judgments of Personality

27. According to evolutionary theory, humans should be able to judge the trait of _____ more accurately than other traits that are less important for the survival of the species.
    a. social potency
    b. social closeness
    c. sociability
    d. sociosexuality

    Answer: d    Page: 111
    Topic: The Accuracy of Lay
    Judgments of Personality

28. Dan's best friend Doug was his childhood friend and his college roommate, and he has known him for over twenty years. Jim has only known Dan since he joined Jim's department at Acme Advertising Agency two months ago. According to Colvin and Funder (1991), if both Doug and Jim are asked to predict how Dan will behave during an ad presentation next week, whose predictions will be more accurate?
    a. Doug's
    b. Jim's

    c. The two predictions will be about equally accurate.
    d. Neither. Such behavior is not predictable.

    Answer: c    Page: 112
    Topic: The Accuracy of Lay
    Judgments of Personality

29. What was the boundary on the acquaintanceship effect identified by Colvin and Funder (1991)?
    a. The advantage of close acquaintances vanishes when the criterion is the ability to predict behavior in a situation similar to one that strangers have seen, but that acquaintances have not.
    b. Judgments made by acquaintances who have known the target five years are equally as valid as judgments made by parents and acquaintances who have known the target twenty years.
    c. Strangers' judgments are more accurate than acquaintances' judgments when the criterion is self-other agreement.
    d. Strangers' judgments, based on five-minute videotaped observations of the target, demonstrated the ability to generalize to situations and contexts that were very different from the original videotaped interactions.

    Answer: a    Page: 112
    Topic: The Accuracy of Lay
    Judgments of Personality

30. Andersen (1984) found that the quality of information affected the accuracy of personality judgments. According to the results of this study, which kind of information would most likely lead to a social impression that corresponded to the target's self-assessment?
    a. listening to the target describe his or her overt behavior
    b. observing the person's behavior at work
    c. watching a five-minute videotaped interaction between the target and an opposite-sex stranger.
    d. listening to the target describe his or her thoughts and feelings

Answer: d    Page: 113
Topic:  The Accuracy of Lay Judgments of Personality

31. The Brunswikian lens model has been used to explain
    a. the process of construct validation.
    b. how to combine available environmental cues to make judgments.
    c. how an individual, through the "lens" of his or herown biased perceptions, constructs a personality trait in another person.
    d. why some traits are visible while others are not.

Answer: b    Page: 114
Topic:  The Process of Accurate Judgment

32. A judge may see a target's behavior, pay attention to the behavior, and use the behavior in his or her judgment about the target's personality. However, for the personality judgment to be accurate the
    a. observed behavior must be relevant to the trait being judged.
    b. behavior must be unusual and distinctive.
    c. judge must have observed the behavior on multiple occasions.
    d. personality trait must be cross-situationally consistent.

Answer: b    Page: 115
Topic:  The Process of Accurate Judgment

# Using Personality Traits to Understand Behavior

## Summary

Traits are useful not just for predicting behavior, but for increasing our understanding of the basis of what people do. This chapter examines three basic approaches to the study of traits. The many-trait approach looks at the relationship between a particular behavior and as many different traits as possible. One technique used in this approach, the California Q sort, assesses 100 different traits at once. The Q sort has been used to explore the basis of delay of gratifi-cation, drug use, depression, and po-litical ideology. The single-trait ap-proach zeros in on one particular trait deemed to be of special interest and its consequences for behavior; it has been used to study the traits of authoritarianism, conscientiousness, and self-monitoring, among other things. The essential trait approach attempts to identify those few traits, out of the thousands of possibilities, that are truly central to understanding all of the others. The most widely accepted essential-trait approach is the Big Five, which lists as the essen-tial traits to understand personality extraversion, neuroticism, conscientiousness, agreeableness, and openness.

## *About the Chapter*

Personality psychology's emphasis on the technology of assessment can sometimes lead to a misleading view of traits. They are often seen as dry, inert, uninteresting properties that lead to a lot of statistical manipulations but say little about human psychology. This a very mistaken view and this chapter attempts to counter it with examples.

As mentioned in the text, what makes personality assessment interesting is its usefulness for understanding behavior. In this chapter I show how traits can be used to understand delay of gratification, depression, and even Fascism, among other important phenomena. The point to emphasize is that the technology of personality assessment has opened windows to our understanding that otherwise would have remained closed.

This chapter plays a particularly important role in my self-appointed mission, described earlier, to sell psychology to students. The only way to show students that personality assessments teach us something worthwhile is by providing examples. That is the purpose of this chapter.

## *Teaching Notes*

There is a lot of material in this chapter, but it is not particularly difficult. However, there are two potential stumbling blocks.

First, when considering what I call the many-trait approach, it is important to not let students get overwhelmed by tables such as 7.2 through 7.5. Even psychologists sometimes get bogged down by paying too much attention to particular correlations or particular numbers. The important task is to learn to look for general patterns that are consistent across all or nearly all the items in the table. I try to show how this is done in the text, and an instructor could also help his or her students in this regard.

Second, the discussion of pseudo-conservatism in the section on the authoritarian personality could stir some controversy. Pat Buchanan once wrote a newspaper column condemning work on the authoritarian personality (which apparently he never read) for "demonizing" the political right. Yet these authors were careful to distinguish genuine conservatism from radical, pseudo-conservatism. This point may be worth emphasizing in lecture. Examples can often be taken from current events. The Republican nominee for president is usually a genuine conservative. Members of groups such as the Freemen, the Michigan Militia, or the Ku Klux Klan are pseudo-conservatives.

## *Reader Notes*

Several selections in Part II of the Reader are directly relevant to the material in this chapter. Included are excerpts from *The Authoritarian Personality* (Sanford et al.) and the original article on the Self-Monitoring

Scale (Snyder). The Shedler-Block article on correlates of drug use is also discussed in this chapter, as is the Costa-McCrae version of the five-factor model of personality.

## Discussion Questions

1. *From the examples in this chapter, which do you find yields the most insight—the many-trait, single-trait, or essential-trait approach?*
2. *Do you know people who abuse drugs? From your experience, what personality traits are associated with drug use? Are these traits a cause of drug abuse, a result of drug abuse, or both?*
3. *Do you know a male student who is depressed? a female student? Would you say their depression is of a different sort? How?*
4. *The concept of the authoritarian personality is half a century old. Is it still useful? Can you think of current examples, besides those in the text?*
5. *Rate yourself or a good friend on the five essential traits of personality according to Costa and McCrae. Do you feel these ratings contain a lot of useful information? What essential aspects of personality do they leave out?*

## Multiple-Choice Questions

1. From a scientific perspective, the central question about traits asks

   a. how personality traits can be used to understand behavior.
   b. what are the important consequences of personality-trait judgments.
   c. how personality traits combine to form our self-concept.
   d. whether different judges of the same person agree about the person's traits.

   Answer: a   Page: 118
   Topic: Using Personality Traits to Understand Behavior

2. A researcher taking the many-trait approach to understanding personality would likely use which of the following measurement instruments?
   a. the California F Scale
   b. the California Q-Set
   c. the NEO Personality Inventory
   d. the Self-Monitoring Scale

   Answer: b   Page: 119
   Topic: The Many-Trait Approach

3. The _____ is a personality assessment device consisting of a deck of 100 cards, each of which describes an aspect of personality. These cards are sorted into categories by the respondent.
   a. California F scale
   b. Self-Monitoring Scale
   c. California Q-Set
   d. NEO Personality Inventory

   Answer: c   Page: 119

Topic: The Many-Trait Approach

4. The most important advantage of Q-sorting is that it
   a. allows the judge to rate the target person consistently high or low on every trait.
   b. does not require the judge to make subtle discriminations between trait ratings.
   c. can only be used by trained clinicians, thus preventing problems that are inherent when laypersons serve as judges.
   d. forces the judge to compare all the items directly against each other.

   Answer: d   Page: 120
   Topic: The Many-Trait Approach

5. The items in the California Q-Set were derived from
   a. factor analysis.
   b. a formal empirical approach.
   c. Allport and Odbert's original list of trait terms from everyday language.
   d. efforts by clinicians to develop items that would describe their real cases.

   Answer: d   Page: 120
   Topic: The Many-Trait Approach

6. When reading a table of Q-sort correlates, the most important thing such tables show is
   a. the general patterns of correlates that emerge.
   b. the exact value of the correlations.
   c. the exact items that are present in the tables.
   d. both b and c

   Answer: a   Page: 123
   Topic: The Many-Trait Approach

**Questions 7 and 8 refer to Table 7.1, following.**

7. The results of Funder, Block, and Block's (1983) delay of gratification study indicate that between the ages of four and seven
   a. almost all aspects of personality are very inconsistent.
   b. many aspects of personality remain consistent.
   c. the personalities of boys remain consistent while those of girls change dramatically.
   d. the personalities of girls remain consistent while those of boys change dramatically.

   Answer: b   Page: 124
   Topic: The Many-Trait Approach

**Table 7.1**

## CHILD Q-SORT CORRELATES OF DELAY OF GRATIFICATION: GIRLS

| Q-Set Item | Age at Personality Assessment | | | |
|---|---|---|---|---|
| | 3 | 4 | 7 | 11 |
| *Positive Correlates* | | | | |
| Appears to have high intellectual | .27 | .51 | .27 | .24 |
| Is competent and skillful | .37 | .28 | .39 | .19 |
| Is planful; thinks ahead | .38 | .28 | .32 | .16 |
| *Negative Correlates* | | | | |
| Has transient interpersonal relationships | −.24 | −.30 | −.31 | −.41 |
| Is emotionally labile | −.39 | −.24 | −.43 | −.07 |
| Is victimized by other children | −.19 | −.17 | −.35 | −.39 |

## CHILD Q-SORT CORRELATES OF DELAY OF GRATIFICATION: BOYS

| Q-Set Item | Age at Personality Assessment | | | |
|---|---|---|---|---|
| | 3 | 4 | 7 | 11 |
| *Positive Correlates* | | | | |
| Is shy and reserved | .40 | .36 | .42 | .51 |
| Keeps thoughts and feelings to self | .41 | .32 | .35 | .51 |
| Is obedient and compliant | .24 | .25 | .53 | .34 |
| *Negative Correlates* | | | | |
| Is vital, energetic, lively | −.39 | −.32 | −.44 | −.40 |
| Tries to be the center of attention | −.37 | −.23 | −.39 | −.46 |
| Is physically active | −.34 | −.15 | −.51 | −.29 |

*Source:* Funder, Block, & Block, 1983

8. In the Funder, Block, and Block (1983) delay of gratification study, ego control was related to delay of gratification in _____ and ego resiliency was related to delay in _____.
   a. both sexes; girls
   b. boys; both sexes
   c. both sexes; boys
   d. girls; both sexes

   Answer: a    Page: 124
   Topic: The Many-Trait Approach

9. According to the text, sex differences in delay of gratification are likely attributable to differences in
   a. hormones.
   b. attention span.
   c. socialization.
   d. temperaments.

   Answer: c    Page: 124
   Topic: The Many-Trait Approach

10. When a study uses rewards that are strongly desired and gives the subjects something to gain by waiting, then
    a. only ego resiliency will be related to delay.
    b. only intelligence will be related to delay.
    c. both intelligence and ego control will be related to delay.
    d. both ego resilience and submissiveness will be related to delay.

Answer: c    Page: 125
Topic: The Many-Trait Approach

11. Joe is a fifteen-year old who abuses drugs on a regular basis. Research using the Q-sort suggests that, as a child, Joe would probably have been described as
    a. quiet and shy.
    b. overcontrolled and inhibited.
    c. easily victimized and rigid.
    d. emotionally unstable and aggressive.

    Answer: d    Page: 125
    Topic: The Many-Trait Approach

12. Jack Block found that 23 year olds who described themselves as being politically conservative were likely to have been described as _____ at age 3.
    a. self-reliant and energetic
    b. easily victimized and rigid
    c. more likely to have developed close relationships
    d. emotionally unstable and aggressive

    Answer: b    Page: 129
    Topic: The Many-Trait Approach

13. Research on _____ addresses important questions concerning the relationship between inner reality and the private self, and external reality and the self as presented to others.

a. authoritarianism
b. introversion and extraversion
c. self-monitoring
d. conscientiousness

Answer: c    Page: 129
Topic: The Single-Trait Approach

14. Erich Fromm coined the term
_____ to describe
individuals who frequently turn
their will over to a higher external authority but enjoy the experience of giving orders to those
who are below them in the hierarchy.
a. "authoritarian character"
b. "politico-economic conservative"
c. "fascist"
d. "anti-intraceptive"

Answer: a    Page: 130
Topic: The Single-Trait Approach

15. Steve is extremely deferential to
his boss. He complies immediately with all orders and never
questions the decisions his boss
makes. In his role as plant supervisor, Steve enjoys giving orders to the people he supervises
and he gets very angry if they
questions those orders. Steve is
probably
a. a Republican.
b. a low self-monitor.
c. an authoritarian personality.
d. both a and c

Answer: c    Pages: 130, 135

Topic: The Single-Trait Approach

16. The California F-scale
a. is the factor analytically derived scale designed to measure the Big Five personality
factors.
b. consists of 100 trait descriptions that must be sorted into
categories by judges.
c. measures the psychological
orientation that was believed
to be the basis of racial
prejudice and political conservatism.
d. assesses the degree to which
individuals repeatedly adjust
their behavior across situations in order to behave appropriately and function
effectively in each new situation.

Answer: c    Page: 131
Topic: The Single-Trait Approach

17. Adorno (1950) claimed that individuals who hold an internally
consistent set of political beliefs
that support institutions and the
traditional social order while
seeking to protect individual
rights, property, and initiative are
_____; those
who show obvious contradictions
between their acceptance of various conventional and traditional
values and who tend to be cynical and punitive are
_____.
a. conservatives; liberals

b. fascists; authoritarians
c. liberals; conservatives
d. conservatives; pseudoconservatives

Answer: d    Page: 135
Topic:  The Single-Trait Approach

18. A frequent criticism of the authoritarian scale is that scores are affected by
a. an acquiescence response set.
b. a negativity bias.
c. the judge's stereotypes.
d. authoritarians' tendency to disagree with any statement.

Answer: a    Page: 136
Topic:  The Single-Trait Approach

19. According to one survey, out of eighty-six possible employee qualities ranked by their importance by employers, seven out of the top eight qualities involved
a. intelligence.
b. agreeableness.
c. emotional stability.
d. conscientiousness.

Answer: d    Page: 137
Topic:  The Single-Trait Approach

20. In order to alleviate the effects of bias in employment testing, employers should use _____ because they typically do not show racial or ethnic differences or biases.
a. aptitude tests

b. ability tests
c. tests of conscientiousness
d. all of the above

Answer: c    Page: 138
Topic:  The Single-Trait Approach

21. The findings of Ones et al. suggest that the elusive motivation variable that distinguishes good workers from poor ones is
a. agreeableness.
b. conscientiousness.
c. emotional stability.
d. ambition.

Answer: b    Page: 138
Topic:  The Single-Trait Approach

22. Julie is a serious and conscientious employee; however, with her friends at Happy Hour on Friday afternoon she is the "life of the party." According to Snyder's theory, Julie would most likely be
a. a high self-monitor.
b. a low self-monitor.
c. high in private self-consciousness.
d. low in public self-consciousness.

Answer: a    Page: 139
Topic:  The Single-Trait Approach

23. Given Snyder's description of self-monitoring, you would expect someone who is a low self-monitor to be

_____ than a
high self-monitor.
a. less judgable
b. more judgable
c. more emotionally expressive
d. less behaviorally consistent

Answer: b   Page: 141
Topic:  The Single-Trait Approach

24. Low self-monitors are more
    likely to be described as
    a. talkative.
    b. self-dramatizing.
    c. having social poise and presence.
    d. independent.

Answer: d   Page: 142
Topic:  The Single Trait Approach

25. Henry Murray, the inventor of
    the TAT, theorized that twenty
    traits or needs were sufficient for
    understanding personality.  Murray's approach to personality is
    similar to the
    a. empirical trait approach.
    b. many-trait approach.
    c. essential trait approach.
    d. hierarchical trait approach.

Answer: c   Page: 144
Topic:  The Essenial Trait Approach

26. Which of the following approaches relies upon factor analytic techniques to reduce the
    many traits in the English language down to few factors?

a. the many-trait approach
b. the single-trait approach
c. the essential trait approach
d. the empirical trait approach

Answer: c   Page: 144
Topic:  The Essential Trait Approach

27. Which of the following reflect
    the structure of personality presently proposed by many adherents of the essential trait
    approach?
    a. neuroticism, extraversion,
       openness, agreeableness, conscientiousness
    b. authoritarianism, fascism,
       conservatism, anti-Semitism,
       cynicism
    c. the traits of the California Q-Set
    d. self-monitoring

Answer: a   Page: 144
Topic:  The Essential Trait Approach

28. The lower your score is on measures of happiness, well-being,
    and health, the
    a. higher your score is on agreeableness.
    b. higher your score is on neuroticism.
    c. higher your score is on self-monitoring.
    d. lower your score is on
       authoritarianism.

Answer: b   Page: 145
Topic:  The Essential Trait Approach

29. One objection to the Big Five is that
    a. the factors are correlated with one another.
    b. it is not clear that the Big Five are five entirely separate and independent traits.
    c. a good deal of information about personality cannot be reduced to those five traits.
    d. All of the above are objections to the Big Five.

    Answer: d    Page: 145
    Topic:  The Essential Trait Approach

30. Cross-cultural research on the Big Five suggests that
    a. the same Big Five are found in all cultures that have been studied to date.

    b. none of the factors appear to replicate cross-culturally.
    c. the central attributes of personality are generally similar in other cultures but there are important differences cross-culturally.
    d. some of the American factors are found in studies using European samples but none of the American factors are found in studies with Asian samples.

    Answer: c    Page: 146
    Topic:  The Essential Trait Approach

# Anatomy, Biochemistry, and Personality

## Summary

Brain anatomy and neurophysiology are both relevant to personality. Observations of animals suggest that the human brain is really three brains in one: a reptilian, a paleomammalian, and a neomammalian brain. This structure suggests that humans and animals have many basic brain functions in common. What we know about brain functioning in humans comes from the observation of people who have suffered accidental brain damage or undergone brain surgery. Damage to the frontal lobes, for example, seems to affect planning, foresight, and emotional regulation. The amygdala is important for emotions, and the two cerebral hemispheres seem to have different functions: the right hemisphere is more intuitive and the left hemisphere is more analytic. For a time, surgery was used on the frontal lobes and other areas of the brain in an attempt to affect behavior, but this did not turn out to be a worthwhile approach. Theories by Hans Eysenck and Jeffrey Gray describe postulated brain mechanisms, such as arousal or inhibitory systems, that affect major dimensions of personality, such as extraversion and anxiety. These theories remain unproven, but provide a useful starting point for theorizing about the relationship between personality and brain function.

Research on the physiology of personality has explored the effects of neurotransmitters such as norepinephrine, dopamine, and serotonin. Other research has examined the effects of hormones—primarily the male sex hormone testosterone and the "stress" hormone cortisol—on personality. The relationship between anatomy, physiology, and personality is complex, but an integrative model by Zuckerman provides a start toward organizing and understanding them by describing the interactions between five levels of psychological and biological functioning.

## About the Chapter

Research in the biology of personality is exceedingly complex and expanding at a rapid rate. Moreover, it is not yet well-integrated, either with the study of personality or within itself. The biological study of personality includes four separate sub-fields, each of which is biological but has relatively little in common with the others. These are the study of brain anatomy, the physiology of the nervous system, behavioral genetics, and evolutionary biology. These four approaches fall into two groups, the first two topics being considered in

Chapter 8 and the second two in Chapter 9. But it is worth keeping in mind, and conveying to students, that these are better described as *four biological approaches* rather than four facets of a *biological approach.*

Much of what passes for research on the anatomy and physiology of personality is about 85 percent biology and 15 percent personality, if that. Very often, complex physiological measures are compared to simplistic indicators of personality such as questionable self-report questionnaires. So it is a mistake to portray the biological approaches as having made great strides, or as having somehow surpassed non-biological approaches. At the same time, it is not possible to ignore biology in the study of personality. Some solid findings are beginning to emerge, and this chapter is a survey of some of the more clear and important ones.

This chapter includes a brief review of the anatomy of the nervous system and the physiology of synaptic transmission. Some students will have been exposed to this material before, either in introductory psychology or biological psychology courses. The material included here is what I judged to be the bare minimum for understanding the rest of the discussion. An instructor with particular interest and expertise in this area could easily supplement my discussion of anatomy and physiology with further illustration and detail.

The chapter tries to attain a balance between an appreciation for the work that has been done in this area and an avoidance of presenting the results as overwhelmingly impressive and persuasive. So far, they aren't. The biological study of personality is still in its very early stages. Much has been accomplished, but much remains to be done. The field is complex, and further progress will require increasingly hard work.

## Teaching Notes

As mentioned above, this chapter presents a bare minimum of detail about the anatomy and physiology of the nervous system. I did not want to duplicate material better handled in a general course on biological psychology. But for an interested instructor it should be easy to present more detail than included here.

The relationship between neurochemicals, drugs, and personality opens up interesting avenues for lecture and discussion. An interested instructor might pick up Peter Kramer's book *Listening to Prozac* and develop a presentation of Kramer's idea of cosmetic psychopharmacology and its pros and cons.

The integrative model by Zuckerman (Figure 8.9) will strike most students as frightening. They certainly should not be expected to memorize it, or even understand it in any detail. I included it in the book to illustrate the different levels of analysis in the study of the biological basis of personality and to show how complex an analysis is required to even begin to show how the different levels are interrelated. A student who grasps those points has grasped the essentials and should be reassured on that point.

A final observation is that in early drafts of this book I included this biological material within the trait section! Notice how many studies in this chapter (and the next) stem directly from the trait approach. On the one hand, a trait (e.g., aggressiveness) is measured, while, on the other hand, a physiological parameter (e.g., testosterone level) is assessed. Then the two are correlated. The close connection between the biological and trait approach is not always recognized, so may be worth pointing out to students.

## Reader Notes

The historical selection by Wells in Section III of the Reader presents an old humoural theory of personality of the Galen variety. This article shows how long-standing is the interest in finding connections between the visible body and the invisible mind. Beyond that, students may find some of Wells's specific examples amusing. An instructor might want to point out that while the basic issue—the connection between the physical and mental self—remains, research methods have both changed and advanced drastically over the past century. The Dabbs et al. piece on testosterone and Zuckerman's review article are up-to-date examples of current findings in the biological study of personality, directly relevant to this chapter.

## Discussion Questions

1. *What do you think of Eysenck's account of extraversion and introversion? Think of the people you know. Is somebody who would rather stay at home with a book than go to a wild party avoiding overstimulation? Is the party goer ordinarily understimulated?*
2. *Psychosurgery has mostly given way to drug therapy. Is this an improvement? Does it make any difference whether a person's behavior or mood is controlled with drugs rather than with surgery?*
3. *If you could take a pill to improve some aspect of your personality, would you do it? Would you still be same person after taking the pill?*
4. *Let's say you are in intense negotiations with somebody. Your adversary takes a pill to make himself or herself more confident and aggressive and thereby achieves a better outcome than you do. Did your adversary have an unfair advantage?*

## Multiple-Choice Questions

1. The _____ forms the core of the human brain and is the basic structure around which the rest of the organ is built.
   a. neomammalian brain
   b. paleomammalian brain
   c. reptilian brain
   d. hippocampus

   Answer: c    Page: 151
   Topic: The Anatomy and Function of the Brain

2. The reptilian brain includes the
   a. limbic system, hypothalamus, and amygdala.
   b. cerebral cortex, corpus callosum, and association cortex.
   c. occipital lobe, parietal lobe, and temporal lobe.
   d. thalamus, amygdala, and cerebellum.

   Answer: d    Page: 152
   Topic: The Anatomy and Function of the Brain

3. The thick outer layer of tissue that is the seat of cognitive activities such as language, planning, and self-awareness is the
   a. cerebellum.
   b. cerebral cortex.
   c. amygdala.
   d. hypothalamus.

   Answer: b    Page: 153
   Topic: The Anatomy and Function of the Brain

4. The case of railroad worker Phineas Gage illustrated that
   a. brain injuries will affect physical but not psychological functioning.
   b. injuries to the brain can affect personality and behavior.
   c. the amygdala has important effects on fear and anger.

d. the right hemisphere is the province of image-oriented, intuitive thinking.

Answer: b  Page: 156
Topic: The Anatomy and Function of the Brain

5. Reports about the remarkable behavioral and personality effects of accidental brain injury in the frontal lobe led
a. researchers to search for additional psychotropic drugs to treat mental disorders.
b. to an increased understanding of the role of the cerebral cortex in emotional regulation.
c. neurosurgeons to perform lobotomies to control maladaptive behavior.
d. all of the above

Answer: c  Page: 156
Topic: The Anatomy and Function of the Brain

6. Recent literature reviews have concluded that the only people who may have been done any good by lobotomies were those suffering from
a. schizophrenia.
b. extreme anxiety and obsessive disorders.
c. sexual perversions.
d. extreme aggressive tendencies.

Answer: b  Page: 158
Topic: The Anatomy and Function of the Brain

7. The right hemisphere of the brain is primarily responsible for _____ while the left hemisphere controls _____.
a. rational thought; intuitive thought
b. verbal skills; analytic thinking
c. emotional regulation; rational thought
d. schizophrenia; mood disorders

Answer: c  Page: 159–60
Topic: The Anatomy and Function of the Brain

8. People who have suffered damage to the right hemisphere of their brain have manifested
a. schizophrenia.
b. obsessive disorders.
c. multiple personality disorder.
d. manic-depressive psychoses.

Answer: d  Page: 160
Topic: The Anatomy and Function of the Brain

9. According to Eysenck, differences between introverts and extraverts are attributable to the functioning of the
a. limbic system.
b. ARAS.
c. hormones.
d. frontal cortex.

Answer: b  Page: 160
Topic: The Anatomy and Function of the Brain

10. According to Eysenck, introverts are _____ while extraverts are_____.
    a. overaroused by the ARAS; underaroused by the ARAS
    b. underaroused by the ARAS; underaroused by the limbic system
    c. overaroused by the limbic system; underaroused by the limbic system
    d. unaffected by testosterone; unaffected by estrogen

    Answer: a    Page: 161
    Topic: The Anatomy and Function of the Brain

11. Ricardo likes to drive fast cars, and enjoys bungee jumping and going to loud, noisy nightclubs. According to Eysenck's theory, it is likely that Ricardo is a(n) _____ whose ARAS causes him to be chronically

    _____.
    a. neurotic; overstimulated
    b. neurotic; understimulated
    c. extravert; overaroused
    d. extravert; underaroused

    Answer: d    Page: 161
    Topic: The Anatomy and Function of the Brain

12. Eysenck linked differences between neurotics and emotionally stable individuals to the functioning of
    a. the limbic system.
    b. the ARAS.
    c. hormones.
    d. the frontal cortex.

    Answer: a    Page: 161
    Topic: The Anatomy and Function of the Brain

13. According to Eysenck's theory, which personality characteristic should relate to greater salivation in the lemon juice test?
    a. extraverts
    b. introverts
    c. neurotics
    d. stable persons

    Answer: b    Page: 162
    Topic: The Anatomy and Function of the Brain

14. Jeffrey Gray proposes that personality results from the interaction of opposing forces, which he terms the _____.
    a. "stop" or inhibition system
    b. approach system
    c. fight-flight system
    d. all of the above

    Answer: c    Page: 164
    Topic: The Anatomy and Function of the Brain

15. Zuckerman has recently integrated a synthesis of current knowledge about brain functions with the concepts proposed by
    a. Galen.
    b. Costa and McCrae
    c. Eysenck and Gray.
    d. Darwin.

    Answer: c    Page: 166
    Topic: The Anatomy and Function of the Brain

16. Galen suggested that there were
_____ basic types of personality
linked to excess amounts of

_____.
a. five; hormones
b. three; neurotransmitters
c. four; bodily humors
d. two; inhibitory neural
mechanisms

Answer: c    Page: 167
Topic: The Biochemistry of Personality

17. According to Galen, an excess of
yellow bile would cause a person
to be
a. depressed and melancholy.
b. cold and apathetic.
c. cheerful and robust.
d. angry and bitter.

Answer: d    Page: 167
Topic: The Biochemistry of Personality

18. According to research by modern
health psychologists, the choleric
or chronically hostile person
seems to be at risk for
a. heart attack.
b. cancer.
c. stroke.
d. all of the above

Answer: a    Page: 167–68
Topic: The Biochemistry of Personality

19. Chemicals that either facilitate or
inhibit communication from one
nerve cell to another are called
a. synapses.

b. hormones.
c. neurotransmitters.
d. inhibitory communicators.

Answer: c    Page: 169
Topic: The Biochemistry of Personality

20. People with chronically high
levels of norepinephrine tend to
a. be anxiety-prone and dependent.
b. be susceptible to Parkinson's
disease.
c. exhibit hypomanic excitement
and restlessness.
d. suffer from clinical depression.

Answer: a    Page: 171
Topic: The Biochemistry of Personality

21. Wayne tends to suffer from
chronic pessimism, is hypersen-
sitive to rejection, worries ob-
sessively, and is prone to sudden
bursts of irrational anger.  Wayne
is exhibiting the symptoms of
a. high norepinephrine levels.
b. serotonin depletion.
c. hormonal imbalance.
d. low dopamine levels.

Answer: b    Page: 171–72
Topic: The Biochemistry of Personality

22. One criticism of the widespread
use of the drug Prozac is that it
a. is currently prescribed only
for norepinephrine depletion.

b. does not appear to affect personality at all.

c. likely causes serotonin depletion.

d. does not produce predictable effects on personality.

Answer: d   Page: 172
Topic:  The Biochemistry of Personality

23. The biological chemicals that are released from the gonads, the hypothalamus, and the adrenal cortex are called
a. synapses.
b. hormones.
c. neurotransmitters.
d. inhibitory communicators.

Answer: b   Page: 173
Topic:  The Biochemistry of Personality

24. Aggressive behavior has been linked to
a. a failure in dopamine reuptake.
b. synaptic decay.
c. high testosterone levels.
d. an estrogen imbalance.

Answer: c   Page: 173
Topic:  The Biochemistry of Personality

25. In one study, male American military veterans were asked about their past behaviors. Those with higher testoterone levels more often reported
a. having assaulted others.

b. having very few sexual partners.

c. problems with depression.

d. experiencing delusions.

Answer: a   Page: 173
Topic:  The Biochemistry of Personality

26. Men with high levels of testosterone
a. are always more aggressive than men with low levels of testosterone.
b. are not necessarily aggressive.
c. are extremely likely to commit aggravated rape.
d. tend to have more education and are wealthier than men with low levels of testosterone.

Answer: b   Page: 174
Topic:  The Biochemistry of Personality

27. The relationship between testosterone and physical aggression holds for
a. relatively uneducated men from low economic classes.
b. very educated men from high economic classes.
c. relatively uneducated women and both educated and uneducated men.
d. all men regardless of education or class background.

Answer: a   Page: 174
Topic:  The Biochemistry of Personality

28. One difficulty researchers experience when attempting to directly link testosterone to aggression and sexuality is that
    a. the relationships have never been studied in women.
    b. testosterone seems to affect sexual desire in men but not in women.
    c. it is difficult to determine the causal direction since aggression and sex can affect testosterone levels.
    d. both b and c

    Answer: c   Page: 175
    Topic: The Biochemistry of Personality

29. Which hormone is sometimes called the "flight or fight" hormone?
    a. testosterone
    b. estrogen
    c. progesterone
    d. cortisol

    Answer: d   Page: 176
    Topic: The Biochemistry of Personality

30. Maria tends to be an impulsive sensation seeker who is disinclined to follow societal rules and norms. Even very dangerous activities do not seem to elicit much of a fear response from her. It is likely that Maria has abnormally
    a. high levels of testosterone.
    b. low levels of testosterone.
    c. high levels of cortisol.
    d. low levels of cortisol.

    Answer: d   Page: 176
    Topic: The Biochemistry of Personality

31. In Zuckerman's hierarchical model of the biological basis of personality, _____ lie at the fifth and lowest level of analysis.
    a. supertraits
    b. emotions
    c. neurotransmitters
    d. reward expectations

    Answer: c   Page: 177
    Topic: The Biochemistry of Personality

9

# The Inheritance of Personality: Behavioral
# Genetics and Evolutionary Theory

## Summary

Behavioral genetics and evolutionary biology both concern how personality might be inherited from one's parents and ancestors. Behavioral genetics addresses individual differences in behavioral traits and examines how parents transmit traits to their children and how biological relatives tend to be psychologically similar. Many personality traits are heritable in this sense, but this finding does not mean that personality is genetically determined. The environment remains critically important. Evolutionary biology explains patterns of behavior that are characteristic of the entire species, such as aggression, altruism, and mating, as being those that have been useful for reproductive success as the human species evolved. Some of these explanations are controversial. But research on evolutionary biology and behavioral genetics does imply that biology and genetic inheritance are involved in the determination of human personality. Biology will never take over the functions of other areas of personality research and theory. As exemplified by Bem's theory of the development of sexual orientation, the promise of the biological approaches comes from their potential to illuminate their interactions between biological, personality, social, and sociological influences on behavior.

## About the Chapter

This chapter covers two very different ways of considering the biological inheritance of personality. The first, behavioral genetics, focuses exclusively on individual differences. Like the trait approach, its research design captures differences between people rather than aspects of personality all people have in common. Indeed, nearly all studies in behavioral genetics are based on assessments of the similarities among relatives according to self-report personality questionnaires.

This chapter presents the basic tool of research on behavioral genetics, the heritability coefficient. This statistic is explained because it is ubiquitous in research on behavioral genetics and even appears frequently in the popular media, but its usage is confusing. Behavioral geneticists all acknowledge that the heritability coefficient is *not* a nature-nurture ratio that quantifies the relative importance of genes versus environment, but the number is often discussed as if that were exactly what it meant. So the chapter cautions against this misinterpretation, which leaves us with this question: What *does* a heritability coefficient mean? In my opinion, it means that, when a heritability of a given trait is greater than 0, which it nearly always is, then the trait is affected by genetic factors in some way.

The second biological approach in this chapter addresses human nature rather than individual differences. The evolutionary biology of personality seems to assume that all people—or at least all people of each gender—are basically the same, and the question is how evolution shaped people to be this way. This approach is controversial, especially when it touches on topics such as sex differences in mating strategies. Psychologists are divided as to the political implications of this work, and the quality of the reasoning that links theory to data. Clearly an evolutionary explanation of a behavioral pattern cannot be directly proven, but research can poke at issues around the edges. Some examples, such as the infidelity-scenario studies, are included in this chapter.

An important issue alluded to in this and the preceding chapter is that of biological reductionism. Some biologically oriented psychologists seem to believe that, in the end, all of psychology—even personality psychology—will reduce to biology. This chapter includes a section arguing against this point of view, basically on the ground that biological and psychological analyses address fundamentally different issues. It concludes with a summary of Daryl Bem's new theory of sexual orientation, and presents it as an example of the kind of analysis that is needed to bring biological and psychological issues closer to each other. Perhaps in the future we will see more analyses like this of other important psychological phenomena.

## Teaching Notes

It would be useful for the instructor to emphasize the difference between a study of personality that focuses on individual differences as opposed to one that focuses on human nature. Behavioral genetics and evolutionary biology provide good examples of the two emphases.

The material on the heritability coefficient might be difficult to teach. The exact psychological interpretation of this statistic is still a matter of debate, and it is commonly used in the literature in ways that cannot be justified. Depending on an instructor's interest and expertise, one might wish either to skip over much of this material in class and simply note the area is controversial, or to go into greater detail about exactly how heritabilities are calculated and what they mean. New studies reporting heritabilities appear in the newspapers all the time, so an instructor who watches for these can bring this current material to class and perhaps spark a discussion of what it means.

A related complication arises with respect to the big news from behavioral genetics, that the shared family environment has little or no influence on personality development. This is an important claim that needs to be taught to students, but it might be premature to teach it as a matter of settled fact. For one thing, the finding is based on data almost entirely limited to self-report questionnaires. Aspects of personality not captured by such questionnaires are not (yet) included in this general conclusion.

Another complication is that many years of research in developmental psychology has documented the effects of family size, poverty, and parental mental illness on personality development. These are all aspects of the shared family environment, and the conclusions of this vast literature have not yet been integrated with the recent conclusions of research on behavioral genetics.

Students with a feminist orientation sometimes find the evolutionary explanations of sex differences offensive. I would recommend that they be encouraged to work through just what they find to be wrong about this approach and articulate their objections as clearly as possible. This could be the basis of a useful and memorable class discussion that— regardless of what the class concludes about sex differences—could result in a solid understanding of basic evolutionary principles.

For different reasons, some students might find the presentation of Bem's theory of sexual orientation to be problematical, but this is a good time to demonstrate, by example, that psychological research and analysis can provide a useful way of looking at topics—such as homosexuality—that so often trigger little more than heated opinions. The Bem theory is included in this chapter as an example—the only example I know of, to date—of an analysis that combines biological and environmental determinants of behavior in a truly integrative manner. The main point I hope students carry away is not any particular view of homosexuality, but of how sophisticated analysis can connect genetic, hormonal, environmental, and societal variables to explain an important psychological outcome.

## Reader Notes

From Part III of the Reader, articles by Bouchard and by Plomin present state-of-the-art expositions of behavioral genetics from two of the most important researchers in the field. The selection on the evolutionary biology of jealousy, by Buss et al., is summarized in this chapter. The paper by Wilson and Daly is one of the more inflammatory pieces I have seen concerning the evolution of sex differences. Finally, Bem's article presenting his theory of the developmental of sexual orientation is included in the Reader.

1. ## Discussion Questions

2. *What is human nature? If your goal is to understand human nature, what topics must you address?*

3. *Do you think your own personality was shaped more by how you were raised or by the genes you were born with?*

4. *If you have siblings, do you think the family environment in which you grew up was the same, or different, from that of your siblings? If different, do you think these differences account for how you and your siblings turned out differently?*

5. *Do you agree or disagree with evolutionary biology's conclu-sions about sex differences? Do you think these differences exist in the way they are described? Do you find it plausible that they could have an evolutionary explanation? Or do you think they are explained as well or better by culture? Why? (Note: If a student argues that culture explains these differences, the class could be asked to explain where culture comes from!)*

6. *Do you think psychology will ever be reduced to biology?*

7. *(Caution with this one:) Do you agree with Bem's explanation of the development of sexual orientation? In particular, do you think "exotic becomes erotic"? Can you think of examples other than those Bem describes?*

## Multiple-Choice Questions

1. The approach that attempts to explain how individual differences in behavior (i.e., personality traits) are passed from parent to child and thus are shared by biological relatives is called
   a. evolutionary biology.
   b. behavioral genetics.
   c. heritability science.
   d. behavioral Darwinism.

   Answer: b    Page: 179
   Topic: The Inheritance of Personality

2. The approach that attempts to explain how patterns of behavior that are characteristic of the entire human species had their ori-

gins in the survival value they had for our ancestors is called
a. evolutionary biology.
b. behavioral genetics.
c. heritability science.
d. behavioral Darwinism.

Answer: a   Page: 180
Topic: The Inheritance of Personality

3. Monozygotic twins share _____ of the genes that vary across individuals and dizogotic twins share, on average, _____ of the genes that vary across individuals.
a. 50 percent; 25 percent
b. 90 percent; 10 percent
c. 50 percent; 100 percent
d. 100 percent; 50 percent

Answer: d   Page: 180
Topic: Behavioral Genetics

4. Behavioral genetics, like trait psychology, focuses exclusively on the inheritance of traits that _____ while evolutionary biology focuses on the inheritance of traits that _____.
a. all humans share; differ from one individual to another
b. vary among groups of individuals; vary among individuals
c. differ from one individual to another; all humans share
d. are species-specific; are individual specific

Answer: c   Page: 180
Topic: Behavioral Genetics

5. The basic assumption of behavioral genetics is that if a trait is influenced by genes, then it ought to be more highly correlated across pairs of _____ than across pairs of _____.
a. genetic siblings; fraternal twins
b. fraternal twins; identical twins
c. identical twins; fraternal twins
d. adoptive siblings; genetic siblings

Answer: c   Page: 180
Topic: Behavioral Genetics

6. If the correlation between the shyness of a sample of dizygotic twin pairs is .25 and the correlation between the shyness of a sample of monozygotic twin pairs is .50, then the heritability coefficient for shyness would be:
a. .25
b. .75
c. .125
d. .50

Answer: d   Page: 181
Topic: Behavioral Genetics

7. The incidence of schizophrenia was measured in both MZ and DZ twins. The correlation between MZ twins was .50 and the correlation between the DZ twins was .30. What is the heritability coefficient for schizophrenia?
a. .80
b. .20
c. .40
d. .65

Answer: c   Page: 181

Topic: Behavioral Genetics

8. According to estimates based on twin studies, the average heritability of many traits of personality is about
   a. .10
   b. .20
   c. .40
   d. .60

   Answer: c    Page: 181
   Topic: Behavioral Genetics

9. Estimates of heritability obtained in studies using non-twin samples indicate that the heritability of personality traits is about
   a. .10
   b. .20
   c. .40
   d. .60

   Answer: b    Page: 181
   Topic: Behavioral Genetics

10. According to some experts, a large heritability index for a specific personality trait can legitimately tell us that
    a. nature matters more than nurture for that trait.
    b. shared family environment exerts a large influence upon that personality trait.
    c. genes matter for that personality trait.
    d. all of the above

    Answer: c    Page: 182
    Topic: Behavioral Genetics

11. If there is no variation in a trait, then the heritability of that trait will be approximately
    a. 1.00.
    b. .50.
    c. .25.
    d. .00.

    Answer: d    Page: 184
    Topic: Behavioral Genetics

12. Recent theorizing maintains that traits with high heritabilities are likely to be those traits that
    a. are very important for survival or reproductive fitness.
    b. have not been important for survival or reproductive fitness.
    c. have no variation across individuals.
    d. both b and c

    Answer: b    Pages: 184–85
    Topic: Behavioral Genetics

13. A limitation of the heritability coefficient is that it
    a. can vary as a function of many different extraneous variables.
    b. does not yield a conceptual understanding of how personality develops.
    c. does not indicate the degree to which a trait is determined by genes as opposed to the environment.
    d. All of the above are limitations of the heritability coefficient.

    Answer: d    Pages: 184–85
    Topic: Behavioral Genetics

14. Isaac inherited a tendency toward sensation-seeking. As a result, he likes to experiment with various dangerous drugs and has become involved with the drug culture. He has recently begun to rob liquor stores with his new friends. Isaac's experiences illustrate that
    a. the inherited trait of sensation-seeking caused him to become a criminal.
    b. the environment is what creates criminal behavior.
    c. there is a link between inherited traits and the environment the person seeks out because of that trait.
    d. none of the above

Answer: c   Pages: 185
Topic: Behavioral Genetics

15. Timothy, as a result of his genes, went through puberty later than his peers. Because he was much smaller than other boys, they tended to pick on him and he fought back to protect himself. As a young adult, Timothy is much more aggressive than most of his peers. The effects on Timothy's personality (i.e., he is aggressive) are
    a. completely the result of his genetic inheritance.
    b. completely the result of his early social environment.
    c. the result of an interaction between the genetic expression and the resulting social environment.
    d. the result of his social environment in adulthood since

genes cannot affect behavior in adulthood.

Answer: c   Pages: 186–87
Topic: Behavioral Genetics

16. According to evolutionary biology, altruistic behavior might help assure the survival of one's own genes into succeeding generations primarily because
    a. if the people who share your genes survive, then some of your genes will make it into the next generation.
    b. altruistic people tend to attract more mates, thereby increasing the likelihood that altruistic people will reproduce.
    c. altruistic individuals take fewer risks than non-altruistic individuals, so they are more likely to survive and produce children.
    d. all of the above

Answer: a   Page: 188
Topic: Evolutionary Theory

17. Across a wide variety of cultures, _____ are more likely than _____ to place a higher value on physical attractiveness.
    a. women; men
    b. introverts; extraverts
    c. extraverts; introverts
    d. men; women

Answer: d   Page: 188–89
Topic: Evolutionary Theory

18. When placing personal ads women are more likely to specify

that the person they are seeking
be _____, while men are
more likely to specify that the
person they are seeking be

_____.
a. younger than them; older than
them
b. the same age as them; younger
than them
c. older than them; younger than
them
d. older than them; the same age
as them

Answer: c    Page: 189
Topic: Evolutionary Theory

19. Kara is placing a personal ad in
the local paper. According to
evolutionary research on mate
selection, Kara will probably
emphasize her _____
when describing herself.
a. physical attractiveness
b. future goals
c. financial resources
d. personality traits

Answer: a    Page: 189
Topic: Evolutionary Theory

20. Kevin is placing a personal ad in
the local paper. According to
evolutionary research on mate
selection, Kevin will probably
emphasize his _____
when describing himself.
a. physical attractiveness
b. future goals
c. financial resources
d. personality traits

Answer: c    Page: 189
Topic: Evolutionary Theory

21. The evolutionary explanation of
sex differences in mate selection
is that
a. men and women are seeking
very different things. Men are
just seeking sex and women
are seeking commitment.
b. the differences are the result
of a biological fluke and will
disappear completely in the
next hundred years.
c. men and women are seeking
essentially the same thing.
Both are trying to increase the
likelihood they will produce
viable offspring who will
survive.
d. the differences are the result
of socialization practices.

Answer: c    Page: 189
Topic: Evolutionary Theory

22. According to evolutionary theory, the reason men tend to be
very concerned about their partner's sexual infidelity is that
a. they are concerned that their
partner will leave them for
another person.
b. they are concerned that they
are not the biological father of
the children they are support-
ing.
c. they are concerned that their
partner will form an emo-
tional bond with another person.
d. both a and c

Answer: b    Page: 191
Topic: Evolutionary Theory

23. According to evolutionary theory, women tend to be very concerned about their partner's emotional infidelity because
    a. they are concerned that their partner will leave them for another person.
    b. they are concerned that their partner will share resources that belong to them and their children with another woman and her children.
    c. they are concerned that their partner will form an emotional bond with another person.
    d. all of the above

    Answer: d    Page: 191
    Topic: Evolutionary Theory

24. The idea that some women follow a different reproductive strategy than most of their sisters is called
    a. the sexy son hypothesis.
    b. taking the reproductive high road.
    c. the adaptive option proposal.
    d. evolutionary roaming.

    Answer: a    Page: 191
    Topic: Evolutionary Theory

25. Which of the following is an objection to evolutionary theory?
    a. Evolutionary theorizing consists of after-the-fact speculations that can't be put to empirical test.
    b. Evolutionary theorists assume that you do not have to be consciously aware of your wish to reproduce for it to determine your behavior.
    c. Evolutionary theorists assume that those behavior patterns that are present today are essentially inevitable and unchangeable because they are rooted in our biology.
    d. All of the above are objections to evolutionary theory.

    Answer: d    Pages: 191–94
    Topic: Evolutionary Theory

26. The assumption of evolutionary theory that everything that exists today exists because it has a necessary effect is sometimes called
    a. structuralism.
    b. humanism.
    c. functionalism.
    d. critical realism.

    Answer: c    Page: 194
    Topic: Evolutionary Theory

27. According to Maryanski and Turner (1992), functionalism has been discredited as a tool of social science primarily because social scientists have recognized that it commits the
    a. theological mistake.
    b. teleological fallacy.
    c. evolutionary error.
    d. deterministic mistake.

    Answer: b    Page: 194
    Topic: Evolutionary Theory

28. The idea that once everything is known about brain structure and physiology we will be able to re-

duce everything about the mind to biology is called

a. the teleological fallacy.
b. biological reductionism.
c. psychophysical structuralism.
d. physiological fundamentalism.

Answer: b    Page: 196
Topic: Will Biology Replace Psychology?

29. Bem's theory of sexual orientation maintains that
a. homosexuality is purely the result of biological variables.
b. sexual orientation is the primarily the result of early socialization practices.
c. the same basic processes underlie homosexuality and heterosexuality.
d. we tend to seek out and be attracted to others who are very familiar to us.

Answer: c    Page: 197
Topic: Putting It All Together: Sexual Orientation

30. An important aspect of Bem's theory of sexual orientation is that it
a. shows what a biologically informed theory of personality should look like.
b. proves what causes sexual orientation in humans.
c. illustrates the interaction of many different kinds of elements to produce sexual orientation.
d. both a and c
e. all of the above

Answer: d    Page: 199
Topic: Putting It All Together: Sexual Orientation

# Introduction to the Psychoanalytic Approach

## Summary

Unlike many other approaches to personality, the psychoanalytic approach concentrates on the cases where the cause of behavior is mysterious and hidden. Psychoanalytic theory is complex, but it is based on a relatively small number of key ideas, including psychic determinism, internal structure, mental energy, and psychic conflict. Of these, probably the most important is the idea of psychic determinism, that everything you think and do has a cause that, in principle, is knowable. Throughout its history psychoanalysis has been controversial, although the nature of the controversy has changed with the times. The theory is truly distinct from the other approaches to personality; it can be regarded as elegant and aesthetically pleasing, and it has had a variety of influences on Western culture. Freud himself was one of the geniuses of the twentieth century. Although psychoanalytically influenced clinical practice is still widespread, academic and scientific psychology has shunned psychoanalysis in recent years. Freud's theory, however, is still an important part of intellectual life on university campuses, most often in the English department.

## About the Chapter

This chapter makes a case for the importance of learning about psychoanalysis and briefly outlines the principal underpinnings of psychoanalytic thought. It includes a brief biography of Freud—the only psychologist so honored in this book. The person of Freud is so closely identified with psychoanalysis that it does not seem possible to talk about the theory in any detail without some knowledge about the theorist,who certainly led an interesting life. Peter Gay's monumental but highly readable biography of Freud (see the recommended reading list at the end of Chapter 13) is an excellent source for more information about both Freud and psychoanalysis.

This chapter concludes by observing that Freud's influence goes far beyond psychology.

## Teaching Notes

When I first began teaching the introductory personality course, I was surprised to learn that the section on psychoanalysis was—for me, at least—the easiest to teach. It takes a real struggle to bring some parts of personality psychology to life for the student, but Freud is easy.

Sometimes psychoanalysis is taught with a close attention to theoretical detail and to disputes among the major psychoanalytic theorists. It is obvious that this is not my approach. For an introductory course, I recommend that, instead, an instructor emphasize examples from daily life

that illustrate psychoanalytic issues (such as the Associated Press story that begins the section—new ones like this appear constantly). An instructor who wishes to go beyond this text might want to present some of Freud's famous cases, which I barely mention. A good source for such cases is the *Freud Reader,* edited by Peter Gay (see Recommended Readings). These cases could be used to bring Freud's theorizing to life or, depending upon the instructor's inclination, to show how psychoanalytic reasoning ventures far from the data and goes fundamentally astray.

If the students in the course include any English majors, they might be asked how psychoanalysis is used in the analysis of literature. Later in the text, I will also claim that most athletic coaches are Freudian. This fact could also be extracted from a class discussion if there are athletes in the room. Finally, after all these years, arguments about Freud still appear regularly in both the professional literature and popular media, material that may also provide points for class discussion.

A final note as the coverage of psychoanalysis begins. Many psychologists—especially but not only those outside the sub-field of personality—have a low opinion of Freud and of psychoanalysis, and sometimes make contemptuous, mocking remarks about both. It is probably already obvious that I will not do this. I have a great respect for Freud and his theory, find it truly insightful, and will present the best case for it that I can in the chapters that follow. An instructor with a strong antipathy for Freud will want to present the opposing side, and the dynamics of such a disagreement between text and instructor could, if properly handled, be highly stimulating and educational for students.

## Reader Notes

Part IV of the reader includes two basic articles by Freud. For this chapter I would assign only the first of these.

## Discussion Questions

1. *Do you hear Freudian ideas used in the way people talk about each other? Can you think of any examples beyond those given in the text?*
2. *Have you heard Freud or psychoanalytic ideas used in any other courses you have taken, in or out the Psychology department?*
3. *When instructors of your other courses have mentioned Freud, have they expressed a basically favorable or hostile attitude? on what grounds?*
4. *What do you think it means about a theorist for people to be still arguing heatedly about his ideas almost a century later?*

## Multiple-Choice Questions

1. The assumption that everything that happens in a person's mind and everything a person does has a specific cause that can be identified is called the assumption of
   a. psychic determinism.
   b. mental causality.
   c. psychological determination.
   d. libidinal functionalism.

Answer: a    Page: 205
Topic: Psychic Determinism

2. The deterministic explanation for the behavior of the prostitute-patronizing city prosecutor, described in the text, would be
   a. that the explanation for the prosecutor's behavior lies in the dynamics of his personality.
   b. that the prosecutor decided to get a prostitute of his own free will.
   c. that the prosecutor's behavior is inconsistent and difficult to predict.
   d. both b and c
   e. both a and b

Answer: a    Page: 205
Topic: Psychic Determinism

3. The nondeterministic explanation for the behavior of the prostitute-patronizing city prosecutor, described in the text, would be
   a. that the explanation for the prosecutor's behavior lies in the dynamics of his personality.
   b. that the prosecutor decided to get a prostitute of his own free will.
   c. that the prosecutor's behavior is inconsistent and difficult to predict.

d. both b and c
e. both a and b

Answer: d   Page: 205
Topic: Psychic Determinism

4.  Jason is playing with his brother's new skateboard. He runs it into a wall and breaks it to pieces. Psychoanalysts would maintain that the destruction of the skateboard was
    a. just an accident.
    b. probably determined by some unconscious desire in Jason to ruin his brother's new toy.
    c. a conscious free choice made by Jason right before he ran it into the wall.
    d. caused by the environmental conditions.

Answer: b   Page: 206
Topic: Psychic Determinism

5.  The assumption of psychic determinism leads directly to the conclusion that many of the important things that go on in the mind are
    a. conscious.
    b. accidental.
    c. unconscious.
    d. the result of free will.

Answer: c   Page: 206
Topic: Psychic Determinism

6.  Unlike other perspectives, the psychoanalytic perspective emphasizes the importance of _____ in determining behavior.
    a. conscious desires

b. environmental influences
c. self-efficacy
d. unconscious processes

Answer: d   Page: 206
Topic: Psychic Determinism

7.  According to Freud, the internal structure of the mind consists of
    a. the oral, anal, and phallic stages.
    b. the id, ego, and superego.
    c. libido and Thanatos.
    d. psychic energy and psychic conflict.

Answer: b   Page: 206
Topic: Internal Structure

8.  The irrational and emotional part of the mind is the
    a. superego.
    b. ego.
    c. libido.
    d. id.

Answer: d   Page: 206
Topic: Internal Structure

9.  According to Freud, the rational part of the mind is the
    a. superego.
    b. ego.
    c. libido.
    d. id.

Answer: b   Page: 206
Topic: Internal Structure

10. The mental energy that makes the mind function is called
    a. id.
    b. Thanatos.

c. libido.
d. sublimation.

Answer: c    Page: 207
Topic: Mental Energy

11. Jenny spends a lot of her psychic energy trying to repress or push out of consciousness her memory of a recent mugging. According to Freud, if Jenny is trying to write a novel, she will find that
a. the repression has created additional psychic energy and that will make her more creative.
b. she has little psychic energy left to spend on her writing.
c. she will be able to easily shift the energy from the memory repression to the novel writing.
d. none of the above

Answer: b    Page: 207
Topic: Mental Energy

12. If you are experiencing psychic conflict, the conflict is between or among your
a. libido and Thanatos.
b. preconscious, conscious, or unconscious minds.
c. id, ego, or superego.
d. psychic energy and libido.

Answer: c    Page: 207
Topic: Psychic Conflict

13. According to the text, the prosecutor's psychic conflict about patronizing a prostitute likely resulted in

a. the ego winning out over the superego.
b. the superego winning out over the id.
c. the id winning out over the superego.
d. the ego winning out over the id.

Answer: c    Page: 207
Topic: Psychic Conflict

14. Tracy has a big test tomorrow. Rationally, she knows she should study for it tonight, but she really wants to go to Gregg's party and enjoy herself. When she considers not studying and going to the party instead, her conscience bothers her and she feels guilty. According to Freud, Tracy is experiencing
a. a fixation.
b. regression.
c. the doctrine of opposites.
d. psychic conflict.

Answer: d    Page: 207
Topic: Psychic Conflict

15. Tracy has a big test tomorrow. Rationally, she knows she should study for it tonight, but she really wants to go to Gregg's party and enjoy herself. When she considers not studying and going to the party instead, her conscience bothers her and she feels guilty so she decides to stay home and study for the test so she doesn't feel guilty. According to psychoanalytic theory, Tracy's
a. ego won out over her superego.

b. superego won out over her id.
c. id won out over her superego.
d. ego won out over her id.

Answer: b   Page: 207
Topic: Psychic Conflict

16. The criticism of Freud's ideas that is most popular today, particularly among academics, is that
   a. Freud placed too much emphasis on sex and sexual energy.
   b. Freud's theory is unscientific.
   c. Freud relied exclusively on controlled, systematic studies.
   d. Freud maintains that behavior is largely the result of rational thought processes.

Answer: b   Page: 207–8
Topic: Unique Aspects of Psychoanalytic Theory

17. The criticism of Freud's ideas that was most prevalent at the time that it was first introduced was that
   a. Freud placed too much emphasis on sex and sexual energy.
   b. Freud's theory was unscientific.
   c. Freud relied exclusively on controlled, systematic studies.
   d. Freud maintained that behavior was largely the result of rational thought processes.

Answer: a   Page: 207–8
Topic: Unique Aspects of Psychoanalytic Theory

18. The psychoanalytic approach posits that the location of the psychological action is
   a. in the interplay between behavior, the environment, and conscious thought.
   b. in the interplay between behavior and conscious thought.
   c. all in the mind.
   d. all in the environment.

Answer: c   Page: 209
Topic: Unique Aspects of Psychoanalytic Theory

19. Psychoanalysts tend to believe that overt behavior and conscious thinking are
   a. the most important factors to study.
   b. largely illusions created by the unconscious mind.
   c. unimportant in themselves.
   d. equivalent to personality traits.

Answer: c   Page: 209
Topic: Unique Aspects of Psychoanalytic Theory

20. The psychoanalytic approach is based on
   a. rigorous, controlled experiments.
   b. therapists' experiences with their clients.
   c. Freud's introspections.
   d. both b and c
   e. all of the above

Answer: d   Page: 209
Topic: Unique Aspects of Psychoanalytic Theory

21. The psychoanalytic approach emphasizes
    a. practical application.
    b. basic research.
    c. controlled experimentation.
    d. drug treatments for disorders.

    Answer: a    Page: 209
    Topic: Unique Apects of Psy-
        choanalytic Theory

22. The American tradition, unlike that in Europe, is for psychoanalysts to be
    a. trained social workers.
    b. psychologists.
    c. medical doctors.
    d. neurobiologists.

    Answer: c    Page: 210
    Topic: Unique Aspects of Psy-
        choanalytic Theory

23. Freud's theory has been called elegant because
    a. it tries to explain so many topics.
    b. all of its diverse pieces fit together and are connected.
    c. it never tries to reduce complex cases to a few abstract variables.
    d. all of the above
    Answer: a    Page: 210–11
    Topic: Unique Aspects of Psy-
        choanalytic Theory

24. According to a survey by Pope, Tabachnick, and Keith-Spiegel (1987), approximately what percentage of practicing psychotherapists report relying to some degree on psychoanalytic ideas?
    a. 12 percent

b. 43 percent
c. 75 percent
d. 95 percent

Answer: c    Page: 211
Topic: Unique Aspects of Psy-
    choanalytic Theory

25. Freud began his career as a
    a. psychologist.
    b. sociologist.
    c. research neurologist.
    d. comparative biologist.

    Answer: c    Page: 213
    Topic: Freud Himself

26. The therapeutic technique that originated with Freud and is most closely associated with Freudian theory is
    a. catharsis.
    b. free association.
    c. hypnosis.
    d. projection.

    Answer: b    Page: 213
    Topic: Freud Himself

27. The therapeutic technique that involves instructing the patient to say whatever comes to mind is called
    a. free association.
    b. systematic regression.
    c. repressed memory recovery.
    d. reaction formation.

    Answer: a    Page: 213
    Topic: Freud Himself

28. Freud found that many of his patients' problems were cured through
    a. the administration of therapeutic drugs.
    b. training them to repress painful experiences.
    c. electroconvulsive shock therapy.
    d. simply talking about their problems.

Answer: d   Page: 213
Topic: Freud Himself

29. The "talking cure" is based on the fundamental assumption that
    a. teaching verbal skills will improve psychological functioning.
    b. talking about your problems generally helps you to deal with them.

    c. repeating positive, inspirational messages to yourself each day will improve your self-esteem.
    d. all of the above

Answer: b   Page: 213
Topic: Freud Himself

30. According to the text, if you were to look for a Freudian on a university campus, where should you look?
    a. the university counseling center
    b. the psychology department
    c. the English department
    d. the school of medicine

Answer: c   Page: 214
Topic: Freud and the English Department

# Structure and Development

## Summary

Freud's psychoanalytic theory posits two drives, a life drive, or libido, and a drive towards death and destruction. Libido is a much more important part of the theory; many modern analysts see it as the only important drive. Libido produces psychic energy, and the story of psychological development is the story of how this energy is focused in different areas at four different stages of life. The main issue for the oral stage is dependency; for the anal stage it is obedience and self-control; for the phallic stage it is gender identity and sexuality; and for the genital stage it is maturity, in which ideally one learns to balance "love and work" and to be productive in both domains. Fixation occurs when an individual gets "stuck" in one of these stages into adulthood; regression is a movement backward from a later psychological stage to an earlier one.

Freud's theory divides the mind into three parts: the id, ego, and superego. These parts correspond roughly to emotions, cognition, and conscience, respectively. Primary process thinking is a primitive style of unconscious thought, characterized by association, displacement, symbolization, and an irrational, uncompromising drive toward immediate gratification. Secondary process thinking is ordinary, rational, conscious thought. There are three layers to consciousness: the conscious mind, the preconscious, and the unconscious. The essence of psychoanalytic therapy, performed through techniques such as dream analysis and free association in the context of a therapeutic alliance between patient and therapist, is to bring the unconscious thoughts that are the source of an individual's problems into the open, where the conscious, rational mind can deal with them.

## About the Chapter

This chapter and the one following present a summary of what I see as the most important aspects of psychoanalytic theory. Chapter 11 includes a presentation of the basic drives, the stages of development, fixation, regression, and the tripartite theory of mind and consciousness, as well as a brief discussion of psychotherapy.

The presentation is *not* orthodox Freud or anything like it, and I do not draw close connections between actual statements of Freud and what is said in this chapter. Many other books are available that do that. Rather, my intention is to present the basic ideas and outlook of psychoanalytic thought in a modern context, and

in as persuasive a way as I can manage. This chapter and the next try to sell Freud to students.

Freud died more than half a century ago, and because he changed his theory often during his lifetime it seems likely he would have continued to do so had he lived another sixty years. Perhaps his new version would have looked like the one in these chapters, but we will never know, of course. In any case, rather than provide a literal rendering of Freud's views, I have presented an interpretation based on those aspects of his theory that, after all these years, I find still persuasive.

The reader will find very little about the Oedipal crisis or penis envy, both important parts of the theory to Freud. I don't find those accounts persuasive, so I de-emphasize them in favor of the parts of the theory I do find persuasive. Other changes in emphasis, similar in kind but relatively minor, will also be found in these chapters.

## Teaching Notes

An instructor who wishes to present the "real" Freud might present lectures based directly on Freud's writings, and some of the controversies he involved himself in. A survey of Freud's major works is missing from these chapters, but an instructor might want to include that in lecture. I say relatively little about Freud's theory of relation between the individual and society, as espoused in *Civilization and its Discontents*, but this could make an excellent topic for a lecture or two.

An instructor might wish to emphasize to students that the material in the text is an interpretation rather than literal rendition of Freudian, psychoanalytic thought. An interesting class discussion might be developed around the question of whether or not this is a good way to teach Freud.

## Reader Notes

I would assign both of the Freud selections in Part IV of the Reader with Chapters 10–12, and save the remainder of Part IV for Chapter 13.

## Discussion Questions

1. *Do you find the psychoanalytic account of development in the text persuasive or not? Why?*
2. *Do you think toilet training is a big deal for children? Does the way it is handled have important consequences for how children develop into adults?*
3. *Research in political science shows that most young adults belong to the same political party as their parents. How would Freud explain this? What do you think is the reason?*
4. *Can you think of any oral, anal, phallic, or genital characters among the people you know? Without naming names, what are they like? How do you think they got this way?*
5. *Do you think dreams reveal anything important about the mind of the dreamer? Have you ever learned something about*

*yourself by analyzing a dream you had?*
6. *Would you go to a psychoanalyst if you had a personal, psychological problem? Why or why not?*

## Multiple-Choice Questions

1. Freud called the fundamental force that was necessary for creation, protection, and enjoyment of life
   a. Thanatos.
   b. the primary process.
   c. libido.
   d. id.

   Answer: c   Page: 216
   Topic: Life and Death

2. The psychoanalytic concepts of libido and Thanatos derive from the
   a. principle of energy conservation.
   b. doctrine of opposites.
   c. Oedipal and Electra complexes.
   d. oral and anal stages of psychosexual development.

   Answer: b   Page: 217
   Topic: Life and Death

3. The idea that the basic tendency of ordered systems is toward disorder and chaos is similar to Freud's concept of
   a. Thanatos.
   b. libido.
   c. fixation.
   d. regression.

Answer: a    Page: 217
Topic:  Life and Death

4.  Allen has just broken up with his long-time girlfriend Katy. According to the doctrine of opposites, how will Allen respond to the breakup?
    a.  He will regress to an earlier stage of development.
    b.  He will switch from being an oral character to being an anal character.
    c.  He will try to find a woman who is a little bit different from Katy.
    d.  He will begin to despise Katy.

Answer: d    Page: 217
Topic:  Life and Death

5.  The _____ is the idea that psychic energy can neither be created nor destroyed.
    a.  doctrine of opposites
    b.  conservation principle
    c.  energy fixation corollary
    d.  theory of internal resource management

Answer: b    Page: 218
Topic:  Life and Death

6.  According to Freud, the process of psychological development is driven by the
    a.  investment and redirection of psychic energy.
    b.  development of key psychosocial relationships with others.
    c.  development of autonomy.

    d.  conflict between the conscious and preconscious mind.

Answer: a    Page: 218–19
Topic:  Psychological Development

7.  The main psychological theme of the oral stage of development is
    a.  jealousy.
    b.  morality.
    c.  control.
    d.  dependency.

Answer: d    Page: 220
Topic:  Oral Stage

8.  Baby Jessica's parents respond to her every need as soon as she cries. Freud would predict that, as an adult, Jessica will
    a.  be well-adjusted.
    b.  be passive.
    c.  rebel against authority figures.
    d.  become sexually promiscuous.

Answer: b    Page: 220
Topic:  Oral Stage

9.  An anal character is consistently dealing with issues of
    a.  dependency and passivity.
    b.  jealousy and sexual identity.
    c.  control and authority relations.
    d.  creation and enhancement of life.

Answer: c    Page: 223
Topic:  Anal Stage

10. During the anal stage, parents insist that the child
    a. exhibit self-control and obedience.
    b. remain dependent and passive.
    c. relinquish his or her attachment to the opposite-sex parent.
    d. be assertive and productive.

    Answer: a    Page: 223
    Topic: Anal Stage

11. Two-yearold Jonathan knows he is not allowed to have a second piece of candy. When his mother is distracted, he takes another piece out of the candy jar just to see if he can get away with it. Jonathan is in the _____ stage of development.
    a. phallic
    b. oral
    c. anal
    d. latency

    Answer: c    Page: 223
    Topic: Anal Stage

12. Stephen's apartment is exceptionally neat and clean while Mary Anne's house is always messy. According to Freud:
    a. Stephen is an anal character and Mary Anne is an oral character.
    b. Stephen is an oral character and Mary Anne has regressed to the latency period.
    c. both have developed fixations in the phallic stage.
    d. both are anal character types.

Answer: d    Page: 224
Topic: Anal Stage

13. The physical focus of the phallic stage is
    a. the penis for boys and the vagina for girls.
    b. the anus for boys and the mouth for girls.
    c. the penis for both boys and girls.
    d. the womb for boys and the penis for girls.

    Answer: c    Page: 225
    Topic: Phallic Stage

14. The basic developmental task of the phallic stage is
    a. the acquisition of gender identity.
    b. the development of self-control.
    c. forming relationships with an opposite-sex peer.
    d. accomplishing learning tasks such as reading and writing.

    Answer: a    Pages: 226
    Topic: Phallic Stage

15. According to Freud, boys and girls figure out what it means to be male and female
    a. by being rewarded or punished for gender-appropriate behavior.
    b. through the process of identification.
    c. during the genital stage of development.
    d. all of the above

Answer: b    Page: 227
Topic: Phallic Stage

16. In the last two years, Marco has had over three dozen sexual partners. Marco has likely developed a fixation in the
    a. genital stage.
    b. oral stage.
    c. latency period.
    d. phallic stage.

Answer: d    Page: 227
Topic: Phallic Stage

17. The genital character type
    a. tends to be sexually promiscuous.
    b. is dependent upon other people.
    c. is psychologically well-adjusted.
    d. operates according to the pleasure principle.

Answer: c    Page: 228
Topic: Genital Stage

18. Josie is married, is expecting a baby, and is successfully balancing those demands with the demands of her career. Josie has probably
    a. reached the genital stage of development.
    b. failed to develop the appropriate gender identity.
    c. neglected to resolve her Electra complex.
    d. allowed her id to dominate her ego.

Answer: a    Page: 228
Topic: Genital Stage

19. The mature, well-adjusted person, according to Freud, has developed the ability to
    a. learn from his or her mistakes.
    b. think logically and rationally.
    c. conquer the unconscious mind.
    d. love and work.

Answer: d    Page: 228
Topic: Genital Stage

20. Joe developed a fixation in the phallic stage. When he experiences a great deal of stress at work, Joe will likely become
    a. disorganized.
    b. uninterested in sex.
    c. dependent and passive.
    d. overcontrolled and anxious.

Answer: b    Page: 230
Topic: Moving through Stages

21. Leaving a disproportionate amount of libido behind at a childhood stage of development is called
    a. regression.
    b. fixation.
    c. transference.
    d. the secondary process.

Answer: b    Page: 230
Topic: Moving through Stages

22. When she is scared, twenty-five-year old Maria becomes very passive and dependent. Maria is experiencing
    a. regression.
    b. transference.
    c. sublimation.

d. libidinal restructuring.

Answer: a    Page: 230
Topic: Moving through Stages

23. The id, ego, and superego correspond to the _____ aspects of the self.
    a. unconscious, preconscious, and conscious
    b. physical, cognitive, and ethical
    c. need, want, and desire
    d. affective, rational, and behavioral

Answer: b    Page: 231
Topic: The Structure of the Mind

24. The _____ brain primarily deals with basic emotions and motivation and is analogous to the _____.
    a. neomammalian; superego
    b. paleomammalian; id
    c. reptilian; id
    d. paleomammalian; ego

Answer: c    Page: 231
Topic: The Id

25. At birth, a baby's mind is dominated by
    a. secondary thought processes.
    b. id impulses.
    c. conscious desires.
    d. ego functions.

Answer: b    Pages: 231
Topic: The Id

26. The ego develops most quickly and significantly from experiences that typically take place during the _____ stage of development.
    a. oral
    b. phallic
    c. genital
    d. anal

Answer: d    Page: 232
Topic: The Ego

27. Modern ego psychologists believe that the primary function of the ego is to
    a. get the pleasures the id wants.
    b. store and enforce rules.
    c. make sense of experiences.
    d. operate the unconscious mind.

Answer: c    Page: 233
Topic: The Ego

28. The superego develops through
    a. the development of fixations.
    b. regression during development.
    c. the process of identification.
    d. primary process thinking.

Answer: c    Page: 233
Topic: The Superego

29. The superego maintains its power through its ability to create
    a. dreams.
    b. anxiety.
    c. psychic energy.
    d. fixations.

Answer: b    Page: 234
Topic: The Superego

30. Unconscious thought is generally due to _____ and conscious thought is generally due to _____.
    a. primary process thinking; secondary process thinking
    b. regression; repression
    c. secondary process thinking; primary process thinking
    d. superego functioning; id functioning

    Answer: a    Pages: 234–35
    Topic: Primary and Secondary Process Thinking

31. According to Freud, symbols in dreams
    a. are the result of primary process thinking.
    b. are a way for unconscious thoughts to become conscious.
    c. have meanings that vary for every individual.
    d. all of the above

    Answer: d    Pages: 235–36
    Topic: Primary and Secondary Process Thinking

32. The largest and most important level of consciousness in Freud's topographic model of the mind is the
    a. conscious mind.
    b. ego.
    c. unconscious mind.
    d. id.

    Answer: c    Page: 237
    Topic: Consciousness

33. The primary goal of psychoanalytic therapy is to
    a. bring unconscious conflicts into conscious awareness.
    b. teach the client to repress id impulses.
    c. regress the client to earlier levels of functioning through hypnosis.
    d. have the therapist become emotionally involved with the client.

    Answer: a    Page: 237
    Topic: Psychoanalytic Therapy

34. One criticism of psychoanalytic therapy is that
    a. it has a low cure rate.
    b. it is effective for schizophrenia but not anxiety disorders.
    c. it focuses on current problems to the exclusion of earlier difficulties.
    d. all of the above

    Answer: a    Page: 238
    Topic: Psychoanalytic Therapy

12

# Defenses and Slips

## *Summary*

Anxiety can have its origins in the real world or inner, psychic conflict, such as that produced by an impulse of the id that the ego and superego try to combat. The ego has several defense mechanisms to protect against the conscious experience of excessive anxiety and its associated negative emotions, such as shame and guilt. These defense mechanisms include denial, repression, reaction formation, projection, rationalization, intellec- tualization, displacement, and subli- mation.

Forbidden impulses of the id can occasionally be expressed in thought and behavior in two ways. Parapraxes are accidental ventings of forbidden impulses in the kind of accidents of speech or action commonly called "Freudian slips." In wit, a forbidden impulse is deeply disguised in such a way as to permit its enjoyment with- out anxiety. A joke is not funny when this disguise is insufficient.

Psychoanalytic theory violates several of the conventional canons of science, but remains valuable because of the questions that it raises and the unique view of human nature that it provides.

## About the Chapter

Most of the comments about Chapter 11 also apply to Chapter 12. I would suggest that they be assigned together. Chapter 12 ends with a summary of the major criticisms of psychoanalysis, along with a defense. The pros and cons of psychoanalysis are numerous and can be the bases of interesting and useful lectures and class discussions.

## Reader Notes

The two Freud articles in Part IV of the Reader may be assigned with this chapter or with Chapter 11.

## Teaching Notes

Students find lectures on the defense mechanisms particularly interesting. It is easy and fun to generate numerous examples, and students can be encouraged to come up with their own. It is also a good use of class time to develop more examples of slips and their interpretation, and to tell some jokes and try to psychoanalyze them according to the theory presented in this chapter.

## Discussion Questions

1. *Do you think you can be anxious about something without knowing what it is? Or does that strike you as a nonsensical idea?*

2. *What examples of the various defense mechanisms—in your own behavior or that of others— can you come up with?*

3. *Athletes in the class: Is your coach a Freudian?*

4. *What's the funniest joke you have heard lately? Can you explain, from a psychoanalytic perspective, what makes it funny? Have you heard a joke lately that you did not find funny? Can you explain what went wrong?*

5. *Do you find psychoanalytic theory worthwhile? Does it seem truly scientific? Does it offer a persuasive account of anything real in your life?*

6. *On what grounds should we decide whether a complex theory like psychoanalysis is worthwhile?*

## Multiple-Choice Questions

1. The primary result of psychic conflict is
   a. depression.
   b. aggression.
   c. anxiety.
   d. immorality.

Answer: c   Page: 240
Topic: Anxiety and Defense

2. Diana, a married woman, is contemplating having an affair with
   an attractive man in her department. How would Diana's ego
   likely respond?
   a. It would encourage her to pur-
      sue the affair immediately.
   b. It would object to the affair
      because it seems immoral.
   c. It would object to the affair
      because it seems impractical.
   d. It would make Diana feel
      guilty.

Answer: c   Page: 241
Topic: Sources of Anxiety

3. Trisha, who is on a diet, passes
   by a bakery and sees a chocolate
   cake in the window. She immediately wants to go in and get the
   cake but then realizes that eating
   the cake will only destroy her
   diet and feels guilty for even
   thinking about breaking her diet.
   Trisha is experiencing
   a. psychic conflict.
   b. delay of gratification.
   c. sublimation.
   d. reaction formation.

Answer: a   Pages: 241
Topic: Sources of Anxiety

4. Which part of the personality is
   responsible for creating defense
   mechanisms?
   a. the unconscious mind
   b. the ego
   c. the superego
   d. the conscious mind

Answer: b   Page: 242
Topic: Defense Mechanisms

5. Strategies that help individuals
   cope with anxiety, guilt, and
   shame are called
   a. compensatory processes.
   b. regressive tendencies.
   c. fixations.
   d. defense mechanisms.

Answer: d   Page: 242
Topic: Defense Mechanisms

6. Zeke has just found out that his
   brother was killed in a plane
   crash. His first response is "No,
   not John, he's not dead." According to psychoanalytic theory,
   Zeke is experiencing the opera-
   tion of a(n)
   a. parapraxis.
   b. fixation.
   c. defense mechanism.
   d. id impulse.

Answer: c   Page: 242
Topic: Defense Mechanisms—
       Denial

7. Brian and Matt have both just
   flunked out of college. Brian is
   sure he didn't flunk and that he
   really is going to graduate. Matt
   simply refuses to think about
   what just happened. Brian is using the defense mechanism of
   _____ and Matt is
   using _____.
   a. denial; intellectualization
   b. rationalization; repression
   c. reaction formation; rationali-
      zation
   d. denial; repression

Answer: d   Pages: 242–43
Topic: Defense Mechanisms—
    Denial and Repression

8.  Ruth is a biology major who hates her current biology class. Which of the following would be an example of Ruth repressing her feelings about the class?
    a. forgetting to bring home the homework for the class
    b. accidentally oversleeping and missing the class
    c. neglecting to call her lab partner
    d. all of the above

Answer: d   Page: 243
Topic: Defense Mechanisms—
    Repression

9.  Angie has completely repressed any memory of the sexual abuse she experienced as a child. Lately, she has been experiencing extreme stress at work and is going through a traumatic divorce. Angie will probably
    a. begin to recall the sexual abuse.
    b. experience a failure of her defense mechanism.
    c. experience anxiety.
    d. all of the above

Answer: d   Page: 244
Topic: Defense Mechanisms—
    Repression

10. The defense mechanism of _____ keeps forbidden thoughts, feelings, and impulses out of awareness by replacing them with their opposites.
    a. parapraxis
    b. projection
    c. reaction formation
    d. displacement

Answer: c   Page: 245
Topic: Defense Mechanisms—
    Reaction Formation

11. One explanation of extreme homophobia is that it is the result of
    a. reaction formation.
    b. displacement.
    c. denial.
    d. rationalization.

Answer: a   Page: 245
Topic: Defense Mechanisms—
    Reaction Formation

12. _____ involves attributing your unwanted impulses and feelings to another person.
    a. Displacement
    b. Projection
    c. Repression
    d. Compensation

Answer: b   Page: 246
Topic: Defense Mechanisms—
    Projection

13. Debbie accuses her husband of having an affair because she is secretly attracted to the next door neighbor. Debbie is likely _____ her own feelings.
    a. projecting
    b. repressing
    c. rationalizing

d. displacing

Answer: a    Page: 246
Topic: Defense Mechanisms—
Projection

14. According to the text, the most
frequently used defense mechanism is probably
a. repression.
b. denial.
c. reaction formation.
d. rationalization.

Answer: d    Page: 247
Topic: Defense Mechanisms—
Rationalization

15. Mark claims that it is okay for
him to take supplies from his
employer because he uses some
of them to do office work at
home. Mark is using the defense
mechanism of
a. repression.
b. denial.
c. rationalization.
d. intellectualization.

Answer: c    Page: 247
Topic: Defense Mechanisms—
Rationalization

16. If you deal with an unpleasant or
threatening feeling by turning it
into a thought, you are using
a. rationalization.
b. intellectualization.
c. repression.
d. reaction formation.

Answer: b    Page: 247–48

Topic: Defense Mechanisms—
Intellectualization

17. Chris spends most of the time
before his surgery calmly dis-
cussing the death rates associated
with the illness and the surgery
with his doctor, reading all the
latest medical articles on the disease, and studying all the surgical
procedures. He views his illness
as an interesting opportunity to
learn more about medicine.
Freud would say that Chris was
using _____
to deal with his illness.
a. denial
b. rationalization
c. repression
d. intellectualization

Answer: d    Page: 248
Topic: Defense Mechanisms—
Intellectualization

18. Dennis is very attracted to his
boss Heidi. Instead of asking her
out, he asks his neighbor Karen
to go out with him. Dennis is
_____ his feelings
for his boss.
a. displacing
b. projecting
c. denying
d. rationalizing

Answer: a    Page: 249
Topic: Defense Mechanisms—
Displacement

19. The defense mechanism of
_____ involves
relocating the object of an emo-

tional response or desire from an unsafe target to a safe one.
a. projection
b. displacement
c. transference
d. transmutation

Answer: b   Page: 249
Topic: Defense Mechanisms—
Displacement

20. Experimental research evidence indicates that a person who displaces aggression will
a. be less inclined to be aggressive in general.
b. be more inclined to be aggressive in general.
c. use rationalization as a defense mechanism.
d. use projection as a defense mechanism.

Answer: b   Page: 249
Topic: Defense Mechanisms—
Displacement

21. The works of Leonardo da Vinci and Michelangelo were, according to Freud, examples of
a. fixation.
b. intellectualization.
c. sublimation.
d. projection.

Answer: c   Page: 250
Topic: Defense Mechanisms—
Sublimation

22. If an woman pursued an acting career because she craved attention and adulation, Freud would probably say she

a. was regressing to the anal stage of development.
b. was sublimating her forbidden impulses.
c. had developed a fixation during the phallic stage.
d. had an unresolved Electra complex.

Answer: b   Page: 250
Topic: Defense Mechanisms—
Sublimation

23. _____ are the result of unsuccessful attempts by the ego and superego to control forbidden impulses.
a. Parapraxes
b. Fixations
c. Defense mechanisms
d. Repressed memories

Answer: a   Page: 251
Topic: The Expression of Impulse—Parapraxes

24. A parapraxis is another name for a
a. slip of the tongue.
b. fixation.
c. repressed memory.
d. sublimation.

Answer: a   Page: 251
Topic: The Expression of Impulse—Parapraxes

25. Dan was in a hurry and forgot to kiss his wife good-bye before leaving for work. Freud would say that
a. the stress of being late made Dan forget.

b. Dan's behavior is a symptom of fixation in the genital stage.

c. Dan may be harboring some form of hostility toward his wife.

d. forgetting the kiss was an accident.

Answer: c  Pages: 251
Topic: The Expression of Impulse—Parapraxes

26. If you commit a slip of the tongue when you are tired, Freud would say that
a. the slip was an accident.
b. the slip was caused by the fatigue.
c. fatigue made it easier for the impulse to be expressed.
d. both a and b

Answer: c  Page: 253
Topic: The Expression of Impulse—Parapraxes

27. Controlled expressions of forbidden impulses are the basis of _____ while uncontrolled expressions are the basis of _____.
a. forgetting; slips of the tongue
b. wit; parapraxes
c. bad jokes; funny jokes
d. projection; displacement

Answer: b  Page: 254
Topic: The Expression of Impulse—Wit

28. In a successful joke, the forbidden impulse is
a. disguised.
b. repressed.
c. obvious.
d. expressed directly.

Answer: a  Page: 255–56
Topic: The Expression of Impulse—Wit

29. One criticism of psychoanalytic theory offered in the text is that it
a. tries to explain too many things.
b. relies on case study evidence.
c. is so scientific that it can't be applied to daily life.
d. bases its theorizing primarily on the experiences of women.

Answer: b  Pages: 258
Topic: Psychoanalytic Theory: An Evaluation

30. Psychoanalytic theory frequently leads to a set of hypotheses that cannot be confirmed by observations. In that respect, psychoanalytic theory
a. is nonparsimonious.
b. lacks generalizability.
c. is untestable.
d. does not use operational definitions.

Answer: c  Page: 259
Topic: Psychoanalytic Theory: An Evaluation

31. One criticism of Freudian theory is that he considers the development of women to be
    a. the basis of male development.
    b. a deviation from the male model.
    c. an example of normal development.
    d. both a and c

Answer: b   Page: 259
Topic: Psychoanalytic Theory: An Evaluation

32. One conclusion that can be made about psychoanalytic theory is that it is
    a. a template for what a complete theory of personality should look like.
    b. an example of the problems associated with basing a theory on experimental evidence.
    c. valuable for the insights it has provided about women's development.
    d. scientifically based and therefore valid and generalizable to most people.

Answer: a   Page: 260
Topic: Psychoanalytic Theory: An Evaluation

# Psychoanalysis after Freud

## *Summary*

Freud died more than half a century ago, but his theory lives on in a variety of ways. Some psychoanalysts try to preserve his theory in its pure form, while other post-Freudians continue to interpret, update, revise, and argue about Freud's basic theory. Others have attempted to develop their own, distinct kinds of psychoanalytic theory. Still others content themselves with debunking Freud without offering a real alternative. Neo-Freudians who have offered theories of their own include such famous individuals as Alfred Adler, Carl Jung, Karen Horney, and Erik Erikson. The kind of theoretical development these individuals worked on seems to have been relegated to the past, however. Modern psychologists interested in psychoanalysis are trying to bring rigorous research methodology to bear on some of the hundreds of hypotheses that could be derived from psychoanalytic theory. Some of these hypotheses seem to have been confirmed, such as the existence of unconscious mental processes and phenomena such as repression and transference. A particularly fruitful area of research has studied the connection between childhood patterns of attachment and adult patterns of romantic love. If more researchers conduct this kind of research, and manage to overcome some significant obstacles, then the future of psychoanalysis could become bright indeed.

## About the Chapter

This chapter covers a lot of ground. It summarizes the fate of psychoanalytic theory since Freud's death in 1939. It briefly describes modern, orthodox psychoanalysis and the never-ending efforts to debunk Freud. Brief summaries of the major neo-Freudians (Adler, Jung, Horney, and Erikson) are included . Modern empirical research relevant to psychoanalysis is described. Many different examples could have been chosen for more extended treatment; I chose modern research on adult attachment theory as most likely to be of interest to a student audience.

## Teaching Notes

This chapter leaves open more possibilities than any other so far for the development of supplementary lec-

tures. Many instructors spend major parts of the course on one or more of the neo-Freudians, particularly Jung and Erikson. Horney is not always included among this company but I recommend her highly. Her books are well-written and accessible, and they address issues that remain relevant today. There is also something to be said for having coverage of psychoanalysis include at least one major female theorist.

My relatively extended treatment of adult attachment theory could be expanded further—the literature is huge—or supplemented by lectures on other relevant, modern research topics. These could include the cognitive unconscious, perceptual defense, the effects of psychoanalytic psychotherapy, and psychoanalytically derived personality types (such as the Jungian types measured by the Myers-Briggs Inventory). Most instructors will also want to indicate whether they think my treatment of Freud was too harsh (few will think that), too lenient, or about right.

## Reader Notes

Section IV of the Reader includes selections by the neo-Freudian theorists Jung, Adler, Horney, and Erikson. The Erikson selection is directly relevant to material in this chapter, but the others are more peripheral. The Reader also includes a report of a remarkable set of post-Freudian studies by Silverman and Weinberger, in which the subliminal presentation of stimuli such as MOMMY AND I ARE ONE alleviated symptoms of mental disturbance. Finally, the Reader includes an angry critique of psychoanalysis by the feminist writer Gloria Steinem. This critique ought to stimulate discussion. If it doesn't, I don't know what will.

## Discussion Questions

1. *Do you think psychoanalysis overestimates the importance of sex? How important and far-reaching are the effects of sex on human life?*
2. *Why has psychoanalysis spawned so many vehement critics throughout its history? Is the theory deeply flawed, or is there something about it—perhaps something true—that people find disturbing?*
3. *How far can psychoanalytic theory be bent and stretched before it isn't psychoanalysis any more?*
4. *Do you find the account of the three styles of adult attachment persuasive? Can you recognize these styles in yourself or people you know? Do you think they stem from child-rearing patterns in the way the theory describes?*
5. *Where, if anywhere, do you think psychoanalysis should and will go from here? Is the theory a mere historical curiosity, or does it have a viable future?*
6. *Was Freud a sexist?*
7. *Have you found learning about psychoanalytic theory to be valuable? Is it relevant to real life?*

## Multiple-Choice Questions

1. Unlike Adler and Jung, most contemporary neo-Freudians
   a. seldom have their own original theories.
   b. hold Freud's original ideas inviolate.
   c. reject most of Freud's theoretical concepts.
   d. place more emphasis on the functioning of the id than did Freud.

   Answer: a   Page: 264
   Topic: Modern Reactions to Freud

2. Most neo-Freudians rely on information from _____ to test or verify their ideas.
   a. controlled experiments
   b. archival and field studies
   c. Freud's original case descriptions
   d. patient histories and introspection

   Answer: d   Page: 265
   Topic: Neo-Freudian Issues and Theorists

3. One difference between the neo-Freudians and Freud is that nearly all neo-Freudians
   a. place more emphasis on early childhood development.
   b. put more emphasis on interpersonal relationships.
   c. adhere to evolutionary theory and emphasize the importance of sex as a motivator.

d. emphasize the importance of unconscious processes in the determination of behavior.

Answer: b    Pages: 265–66
Topic: Neo-Freudian Issues and Theorists

4.  Adler felt that _____ was the prime motivator of human thought and behavior.
    a. the collective unconscious
    b. animus
    c. social interest
    d. anxiety

Answer: c    Page: 266
Topic: Neo-Freudian Issues and Theorists

5.  Tom was a sickly child and always felt helpless. According to Adler, as an adult he will probably
    a. be a complete invalid.
    b. lose all interest in his social environment.
    c. attempt to overcompensate.
    d. become obsessed with his persona.

Answer: c    Page: 266
Topic: Inferiority and Compensation: Adler

6.  Jane feels inferior to the people around her but she tries to act like she is powerful and in control. Adler would say that Jane is
    a. experiencing the masculine protest.
    b. expressing her animus.
    c. developing a persona.

d. obsessed with penis envy.

Answer: a    Page: 266
Topic: Inferiority and Compensation: Adler

7.  In order for a person to develop an inferiority complex they must
    a. actually have some disability that makes them inferior to others.
    b. perceive that they are inferior to others.
    c. have parents who pushed them to be perfect.
    d. all of the above

Answer: b    Page: 266
Topic: Inferiority and Compensation: Adler

8.  Jung believed that as the result of history we all share inborn species-specific ideas and memories. This is Jung's idea of
    a. social interests.
    b. collective unconscious.
    c. anima.
    d. generativity.

Answer: b    Page: 267
Topic: The Collective Unconscious . . . Jung

9.  The recurring images that are repeated in dreams, myths, and literature throughout the world are called
    a. id prototypes.
    b. animus and anima.
    c. personas.
    d. archetypes.

Answer: d   Page: 267

Topic: The Collective Unconscious . . . Jung

10. Paul is always concerned about how he appears to others so he keeps most aspects of himself hidden and puts on a carefully chosen public face in every situation. According to Jung, Paul has
a. effectively mediated between his animus and anima.
b. become obsessed with his persona.
c. created a false archetype.
d. overcompensated for his sense of inferiority.

Answer: b   Page: 267
Topic: The Collective Unconscious . . . Jung

11. Mike's prototypical woman is sensitive and intelligent. Mike's idealized image of a woman is his
a. unconscious compensation.
b. animus.
c. anima.
d. feminine persona.

Answer: c   Pages: 267–68
Topic: The Collective Unconscious . . . Jung

12. The idea that men and women each have a masculine and a feminine side is linked to Jung's ideas about
a. intimacy and isolation.
b. inferiority and compensation.

c. the collective unconscious.
d. animus and anima.

Answer: d   Page: 267–68
Topic: The Collective Unconscious . . . Jung

13. Jung's distinction between people who are outwardly oriented toward the world and those who are turned in on themselves corresponds to
a. Erikson's stage of intimacy vs. isolation.
b. Freud's ideas of the oral and anal character types.
c. his concepts of animus and anima.
d. a dimension of the Big Five.

Answer: d   Page: 268
Topic: The Collective Unconscious . . . Jung

14. The Myers-Briggs Type Indicator measures
a. the Jungian classification of the four basic ways of thinking.
b. your prototypical images of women and men.
c. the functioning of archetypes.
d. aspects of Erikson's psychosocial stages of development.

Answer: a   Page: 268
Topic: The Collective Unconscious . . . Jung

15. Horney's major deviation from traditional Freudian ideas was her
a. emphasis on anxiety.
b. view of penis envy.

c. ideas about the development of neurotic needs.
d. link between adult functioning and childhood struggles.

Answer: b   Page: 269
Topic: Feminine Psychology and
   Basic Anxiety: Horney

16. Adult behavior, according to Horney, is based on efforts to
   a. overcome the fear of being alone in a hostile world.
   b. deal with recurring Oedipal crises.
   c. resolve interpersonal conflicts with significant others.
   d. repress the collective unconscious.

Answer: a   Page: 269
Topic: Feminine Psychology and
   Basic Anxiety: Horney

17. Horney felt that if women experienced penis envy that it symbolized
   a. their desire to actually possess a penis.
   b. women's lack power and control.
   c. rejection of motherhood.
   d. dissatisfaction with their own bodies.

Answer: b   Page: 269
Topic: Feminine Psychology and
   Basic Anxiety: Horney

18. Erikson's major deviation from Freud included his ideas about
   a. the functioning of the id and the physical location of libido.

b. development as occurring in a series of stages.
   c. the function of the ego and the role of conscious conflict.
   d. the importance of parents to a child's development.

Answer: c   Page: 269–70
Topic: Psychosocial Development: Erikson

19. Freud's anal stage corresponds to Erikson's stage of
   a. generativity vs. stagnation.
   b. basic trust vs. mistrust.
   c. initiative vs. guilt.
   d. autonomy vs. shame and doubt.

Answer: d   Page: 269–70
Topic: Psychosocial Development: Erikson

20. In Erikson's view, important aspects of psychological development
   a. occur primarily in early childhood.
   b. continue to change throughout the lifespan.
   c. are dependent upon the resolution of the Oedipal complex.
   d. involve the investment of the libido at each stage.

Answer: b   Page: 271
Topic: Psychosocial Development: Erikson

21. In middle age, we experience the psychosocial crisis of
   a. generativity vs. stagnation.

b. intimacy vs. isolation.
c. integrity vs. despair.
d. industry vs. inferiority.

Answer: a    Page: 271
Topic: Psychosocial Development: Erikson

22. Ellen is a fifty-year old woman who is raising her two grandchildren, is active in her community, and is learning how to paint. Ellen has chosen
a. industry.
b. initiative.
c. integrity.
d. generativity.

Answer: d    Page: 271
Topic: Psychosocial Development: Erikson

23. According to Erikson, in adolescence all normal teenagers should experience
a. an inferiority complex.
b. a struggle for intimacy.
c. an identity crisis.
d. a sense of shame and doubt.

Answer: c    Page: 273
Topic: Psychosocial Development: Erikson

24. In Erikson's scheme, we progress from one crisis to another according to
a. processes of physical maturation.
b. developmental tasks at different times of life.
c. the successful repression of inappropriate id impulses.

d. the physical location of libido at each stage.

Answer: b    Page: 271
Topic: Psychosocial Development: Erikson

25. Modern developmental psychology has been most influenced by Erikson's idea that development
a. occurs in stages.
b. is influenced by parents.
c. happens across the lifespan.
d. is dependent upon physical maturation.

Answer: c    Page: 271
Topic: Psychosocial Development: Erikson

26. Which of the following might be described as psychoanalytic research?
a. a study of the cognitive origins of aggressive behavior
b. a study to determine the impact of early childrearing practices on adult personality characteristics
c. a study of the role of defensive optimism in maintaining health
d. all of the above

Answer: d    Page: 273
Topic: Modern Psychoanalytic Research

27. Which of the following Freudian ideas is not supported by modern research?
a. repression works as a defense mechanism

b. the Oedipal crisis occurs in
the phallic stage
c. most of what the mind does is
unconscious
d. all of the above

Answer: b   Page: 274
Topic: Modern Psychoanalytic
Research

28. The psychological goal of attachment is to
a. feel secure.
b. sexually possess the parent.
c. avoid conflict with authority
figures.
d. manipulate others.

Answer: a   Pages: 275
Topic: Attachment and Romantic Love

29. Research suggests that anxious-
ambivalent children will grow up
to be adults who tend to
a. be obsessed with their romantic partners.
b. be relatively uninterested in
romantic relationships.

c. have high self-esteem and
confidence.
d. enjoy long, stable romantic
relationships.

Answer: a   Pages: 278
Topic: Attachment and Romantic Love

30. The Freudian element that has
been maintained in modern attachment theory and research is
that
a. attachments can only form
between mothers and infants.
b. the attachment bond is formed
by the caregiver meeting the
child's oral needs.
c. early relationships with parents form models for later
romantic attachments.
d. attachment styles are determined by successful resolution of the Oedipal crisis.

Answer: c   Page: 279
Topic: Attachment and Romantic Love

14

# Existence, Experience, and Free Will: The Phenomenological Approach

## Summary

The phenomenological approach to personality concentrates on the experience, or phenomenology, of being alive and aware from moment to moment. This emphasis makes the approach humanistic, because it concentrates on that which makes the study of humans different from the study of objects or animals. The phenomenological approach asserts that each moment of experience is all that matters, an assertion that implies that individuals have free will, and that the only way to understand another person is to understand his or her experi-

**113**

ence of the world. The approach has philosophical roots in existentialism, which breaks experience into three parts (of the world, of others, and of one's own experience), claims that a close analysis of existence implies that it has no meaning beyond what we give it, and concludes that a failure to face this fact constitutes living in bad faith. As an alternative, existentialism prescribes living an authentic existence, which entails coming to terms with existential dilemmas and taking responsibility for one's choices in life.

Modern humanist psychologists, such as Rogers, Maslow, and Kelly, are more optimistic than their existentialist forebears. Rogers and Maslow assert that a person who faces his or her experience directly can become a fully functioning person; Rogers believed this outcome could only occur for individuals who had received unconditional positive regard from the important people in their lives. Kelly's theory says that each person's experience of the world is organized by a unique set of personal constructs, or general themes. Scientific paradigms have much in common with these personal constructs. Csikszentmihalyi's recent theory says that the best state of existence is to be in a state of flow, in which challenges and capabilities are well balanced. Although modern humanistic psychology continues to maintain that the rest of psychology makes a fundamental mistake by ignoring that which makes humans unique among objects of study, the field has so far offered only non-rigorous, introspective accounts, which psychologists with a scientific

approach find unconvincing. Humanistic psychologists and philosophers still have not settled the issue of whether directly confronting the facts of one's existence should make you happy or miserable. Nevertheless, they must be given credit for providing the only approach that even attempts to address the mystery of human experience and awareness. The phenomenological approach has had an important impact on the practice of psychotherapy, on modern cognitive views of personality, and on the study of psychology across cultures.

## About the Chapter

The term humanistic psychology is often used, but it is not always clear what it means. The interpretation offered in this chapter is that humanistic psychology is an approach rooted in existential philosophy, especially existentialism's emphasis on phenomenology. This trio of multisyllabic terms—existentialism, phenomenology, and humanism—may seem forbidding at first, but the chapter tries to present the essence of each concept and their interrelations as clearly as possible.

I have already become aware that some humanistic psychologists are less than completely happy with their portrayal in this chapter. It is true that so-called humanists disagree among themselves perhaps more than adherents to any other approach (I mention this diversity of outlook near the beginning of the chapter), and so cannot all be tarred with the same brush. Still, I think the present analysis does as well as any other at finding and tying together the common threads that underlie humanism, phenomenology, and existentialism. A particular challenge was to unite Sartre's gloom with Rogers's and Maslow's optimism. I did this by invoking Kelly's personal construct theory. You can judge for yourself how successful this maneuver was.

## Teaching Notes

One challenge in teaching this material is to find a way for students not to be immediately turned off by the philosophic terminology. It helps, I think, to emphasize that existentialism concerns the meaning of life, that phenomenology concerns how it feels to be alive, and that humanism emphasizes whatever is seen as distinctive about humanity.

This chapter probably contains enough existential philosophy for any personality course. An interested instructor with relevant expertise might wish to expand on the treatment of Rogers, Maslow, or Kelly. In particular, Rogers continues to influence the practice of psychotherapy. Maslow's theory is widely applied to industrial settings (e.g., in models of worker motivation). Kelly's phenomenological approach is an important underpinning of the modern cognitive approaches to be considered in later chapters (Walter Mischel was a student of Kelly). All of these points would be worth emphasizing and expanding in lecture.

## Reader Notes

Section V of the Reader begins with a surprisingly readable primer on existential philosophy by Jean-Paul Sartre. The presentation of Sartre in this chapter of the text is largely based on this chapter of the Reader. The Reader also includes selections by the humanists Maslow, Kelly, and Rogers, all of whom are discussed in this chapter. This chapter considers Csikszentmihalyi's theory of flow, and an excerpt from his book on the subject is included in the Reader. Perhaps the most unusual selection in the reader is the piece by Gordon Allport, whose role as an important humanistic theorist seems almost forgotten by modern psychologists. Allport is not mentioned in Chapter 14.

## Discussion Questions

1. *Do people have free will? Or are they driven by their reinforcement history, unconscious motivations, and trait structures? If free will exists, what exactly does this mean, and how is it possible?*

2. *What does it feel like to be alive and aware? Can it be described in words? Can psychology address this experience? How?*

3. *How can a person decide between right and wrong? Is there some authority we can turn to? (If someone mentions God): How do you decide what God wants you to do? How do you decide*

whether or not to obey God? (Needless to say, be careful with this line of discussion—it can be emotionally loaded for many students.)

4. Sartre believed God does not exist, but said that even if God did exist it wouldn't matter. What did Sartre mean by this?

5. How do you think Rogers and Maslow were able to start with existentialist ideas and develop such optimistic-sounding psychologies?

6. If a psychotherapist is treating a murderer or child molester, do you think the therapist should give the client unconditional positive regard? Why or why not?

7. The text discusses opportunity costs as one construct about the world often treated as though it were real. Can you think of other commonly used concepts, treated as real, that can also be thought of in other ways?

8. Would you spend your whole life in flow if you could?

## Multiple-Choice Questions

1. Your unique, individual experience of the world is called your
   a. humanism.
   b. phenomenology.
   c. Umwelt.
   d. existentialism.

   Answer: b    Page: 283
   Topic: Experience and Awareness

2. Adherents to the phenomenological approach believe that
   a. behavior is primarily determined by early events.
   b. to understand the individual, you must understand his or her unconscious and hidden motives.
   c. the methods that are used to study other scientific phenomena can be applied to the study of the mind.
   d. the study of the human mind is affected by human awareness.

   Answer: d    Pages: 285–86
   Topic: A Humanistic Psychology

3. Phenomenological, existential, and humanistic psychologists all agree that
   a. psychology should focus on conscious experience.
   b. the study of human beings is fundamentally different from the study of anything else.
   c. human beings possess free will.
   d. all of the above

   Answer: d    Page: 286
   Topic: A Diverse Approach

4. The phenomenological approach claims that your behavior is the result of your
   a. history of reinforcement.
   b. future aspirations and goals.
   c. immediate conscious experience.
   d. cultural traditions.

Answer: c    Page: 287
Topic: Awareness is Everything

5. Trait, psychoanalytic, and behavioral psychologists agree that behavior is _____
   while phenomenologists claim it is _____.
   a. determined; freely chosen
   b. motivated by unconscious desires; driven by conscious motives
   c. inconsistent; consistent
   d. caused by external factors; caused by internal states

Answer: a    Page: 288
Topic: Free Will

6. Your particular freely chosen interpretations of reality are called your
   a. Mitwelt.
   b. construals.
   c. needs.
   d. experiential definitions.

Answer: b    Page: 288
Topic: Free Will

7. According to the phenomenological perspective, to understand another person you must understand his or her
   a. unconscious desires.
   b. goals and aspirations.
   c. construals.
   d. Mitwelt.

Answer: c    Page: 288
Topic: Understanding Others

8. One possible interpretation of the basic phenomenological philosophy is that
   a. objective reality exists for diverse groups of people and different cultures.
   b. all interpretations of reality are equally valid.
   c. if you look at the world through another's eyes you will realize your own world view is invalid.
   d. our behavior, thoughts, and feelings are determined by past experience.

Answer: b    Page: 289
Topic: Understanding Others

9. The key existential question is:
   a. What is the meaning of existence?
   b. What is the nature of existence?
   c. How does existence feel?
   d. All of the above are key questions.

Answer: d    Page 289
Topic: Existentialism

10. _____ consists of your biological experiences and _____ consists of your psychological experiences.
   a. Umwelt; Eigenwelt
   b. Mitwelt; Umwelt
   c. Eigenwelt; Mitwelt
   d. Umwelt; Mitwelt

Answer: a    Pages: 289–90
Topic: Three Parts of Experience

11. Carolyn is fondly thinking about her mother. Carolyn is experiencing
    a. self-actualization.
    b. Mitwelt.
    c. Eigenwelt.
    d. Angst.

    Answer: b    Page: 290
    Topic:  Three Parts of Experience

12. The time, place, and circumstances into which you were born is called your
    a. existential location.
    b. Eigenwelt.
    c. thrown-ness.
    d. Angst.

    Answer: c    Page: 290
    Topic:  "Thrown-ness" and Angst

13. Jerry has been wondering what life means and whether he is living his life purposefully.  If he cannot answer these questions, he will probably experience
    a. Eigenwelt.
    b. thrown-ness.
    c. Angst.
    d. self-actualization.

    Answer: c    Page: 291
    Topic:  "Thrown-ness" and Angst

14. _____ is the anxiety that results from contemplation of existential concerns.
    a. Thrown-ness
    b. Umwelt
    c. Construal
    d. Angst

    Answer: d    Page: 291
    Topic:  "Thrown-ness" and Angst

15. Mike thinks that sitting around contemplating the meaning of existence is a waste of time.  He spends his life concentrating on developing his career, building a bigger house for his family, and enjoying himself.  Sartre and other existentialists would say Mike is
    a. living in bad faith.
    b. a fully-functioning person.
    c. striving to meet his social needs.
    d. unlikely to experience flow.

    Answer: a    Page: 291
    Topic:  Bad Faith

16. Existentialists would say that if Donna doesn't worry about existential concerns but instead focuses on getting a job, establishing relationships with others, and raising her family she will
    a. become a fully-functioning person.
    b. experience authentic existence.
    c. still not be happy.
    d. feel Angst.

    Answer: c    Page: 292
    Topic:  Bad Faith

17. Steven has come to terms with his mortality, accepted responsibility for his existence, and knows that he determines what happens in his life.  Existentialists would say that Steven is

a. living in bad faith.
b. experiencing thrown-ness.
c. attaining authentic existence.
d. achieving Mitwelt.

Answer: c    Page: 293
Topic: Authentic Existence

18. According to Sartre, the existential challenge is to
a. avoid thinking about the meaning of existence.
b. face the basic uncertainty and anguish of life and find meaning.
c. maintain generativity and avoid stagnation.
d. become a fully-functioning, self-actualizing person.

Answer: b    Page: 293
Topic: Authentic Existence

19. Carl Rogers maintained that the one basic tendency for humans was to
a. maintain and enhance life.
b. struggle against despair and anguish.
c. identify personal constructs.
d. develop conditions of worth.

Answer: a    Page: 294
Topic: Existential Optimism: Rogers and Maslow

20. Rogers' idea of actualization is similar to Freud's concept of
a. Thanatos.
b. ego.
c. libido.
d. intellectualization.

Answer: c    Page: 294
Topic: Existential Optimism: Rogers and Maslow

21. Linda thinks that her friends will only like her if she is thin, attractive, and cheerful. Rogers would say that it is unlikely that Linda will
a. develop conditions of worth.
b. become a fully-functioning person.
c. build personal constructs.
d. experience Angst.

Answer: b    Page: 295
Topic: Existential Optimism: Rogers and Maslow

22. To avoid developing conditions of worth, a person should experience _____ from the important people in his or her life.
a. unconditional positive regard
b. Mitwelt
c. conditions of worth
d. existential optimism

Answer: a    Page: 295
Topic: Existential Optimism: Rogers and Maslow

23. The fundamental belief of humanism is that
a. unconscious experience determines behavior.
b. people are basically good.
c. human beings are superior to other organisms.
d. accurate perceptions of the world cause neurotic distortions.

Answer: b    Page: 295
Topic: Existential Optimism:
Rogers and Maslow

24. The theories of Rogers and
Maslow imply that if you leave
human beings alone then they
will
a. develop into healthy and
happy people.
b. suffer anguish and despair.
c. develop conditions of worth.
d. experience neurotic distortions of the world.

Answer: a    Page: 295
Topic: Existential Optimism:
Rogers and Maslow

25. Research findings indicate that
one result of Rogerian psychotherapy may be that
a. people become more like their
ideal self.
b. people establish their own
conditions of worth.
c. clients report feeling more despair and anguish.
d. most clients achieve self-
actualization through therapy.

Answer: a    Page: 296
Topic: Existential Optimism:
Rogers and Maslow

26. One difficulty in determining the
effect of Rogerian psychotherapy
is that
a. it is not clear that the match
between perceived self and
ideal self is an adequate criteria for psychological adjustment.

b. the criterion used for determining adjustment could lead
us to perceive people with
obvious disorders as being
well-adjusted.
c. the results may be due to clients' changing their ideal
views.
d. All of the above are difficulties.

Answer: d    Pages: 296–97
Topic: Existential Optimism:
Rogers and Maslow

27. Kelly's personal construct theory
emphasizes that individuals
a. construct reality through neurotic distortions.
b. build our experience of reality
through unique sets of ideas
about the world.
c. construct a hierarchy of needs
that motivate behavior.
d. build an authentic existence
through the acceptance of
personal responsibility.

Answer: b    Page: 297
Topic: Personal Constructs:
Kelly

28. A personality test that asks you to
identify sets of three people,
ideas, or objects and then has you
describe how any two of them are
similar to each other and different from the third is attempting to
assess your
a. hierarchy of needs.
b. conditions of worth.
c. cognitive scripts.
d. personal constructs.

Answer: d   Page: 297
Topic: Personal Constructs:
Kelly

29. Csikszentimihalyi's concept of
flow is analogous to
a. self-actualization.
b. an authentic existence.
c. an optimal experience.
d. existential optimism.

Answer: c   Page: 301
Topic: Flow: Csikszentimihalyi

30. You are most likely to experience
flow if the activity you are doing
is
a. easy.
b. confusing.
c. challenging.
d. boring.

Answer: c   Page: 301
Topic: Flow: Csikszentimihalyi

31. Research indicates that experiencing flow tends to:
a. elevate mood.
b. create anxiety.
c. slow metabolism.
d. decrease activity levels.

Answer: a   Page: 301
Topic: Flow: Csikszentimihalyi

32. Currently, humanistic research
most frequently consists of
a. experimental examinations of
construals.
b. subjective analyses of experience.
c. correlational field studies.
d. systematic behavior analysis.

Answer: b   Pages: 302–4
Topic: Humanistic Psychology
Today

33. Phenomenologists tend to disagree amongst themselves about:
a. the existence of free will.
b. the importance of immediate
experience.
c. whether or not awareness
makes the human mind
unique.
d. whether the human condition
is basically positive or negative.

Answer: d   Pages: 304–5
Topic: On Happiness

**15**

# Cultural Variation in Experience, Behavior, and Personality

## Summary

If, as the phenomenologists claim, a person's construal of the world is all-important, a logical next question concerns the ways in which such construals of reality vary across different cultures. This topic is addressed by cross-cultural psychology. It is important to know whether psychological research and theorizing that originates in one culture can be applied to another, because misunderstandings across cultures can lead to conflict and even war, and because to understand how other peoples view reality can expand our own understanding of the world. Hazards of cross-cultural research include ethnocentrism, outgroup bias, and the unfortunate fact that ultimately one person can never fully comprehend the experience of another.

Some psychologists ignore cross-cultural issues. A second group, the deconstructionists, argues that comparing cultures is impossible; we must seek to understand each culture in its own terms. Some deconstructionists have even claimed that the Western sense of self is a cultural artifact. A third group of psychologists follows a comparative approach, contrasting etics, or elements that all cultures have in common, with emics, or elements that make them different. Cultures have been compared on emic dimensions including complexity, tightness, and collectivism. Deconstructionists avoid the question of where these differences originate, but one comparative approach sees the ultimate origin of cultural differences in the differing ecologies to which groups around the world must adapt. Despite the importance of cross-cultural psychology, it is important to bear in mind that individuals vary within as well as across cultures, that cultural relativism can be taken too far, and that beneath all cultural differences there may be a universal human condition in an existential sense: the need to exist, to work, to relate to other people, and ultimately to die.

## About the Chapter

The location of this chapter, in the same section as humanistic psychology, is somewhat unusual. But I believe that the essential aspect of humanism is its phenomenological orientation, and that the basic question of cross-cultural psychology is also phenomenological: Do members of different cultures see the world in a fundamentally different way? The continuation of the phenomenological theme across Chapters 14 and 15 is what ties them together. And to bring the presentation full circle, Chapter 15 ends with a quote from Jean-Paul Sartre, considered at the beginning of Chapter 14.

## Teaching Notes

This is material that students usually find interesting. A point I have learned to keep in mind when teaching this material is that it is too easy to spend one's lecture time talking about abstractions. The comparability of cultures, phenomenology, and deconstructionism versus realism are all interesting ideas that can be developed at length. But if these issues are overemphasized one can finish the cross-cultural part of the course without having mentioned an actual difference between cultures! For this reason, in every revision of this chapter I found myself putting in more specific examples of cross-cultural variation, and I try to remember to do the same in lecture.

I am no world traveler but have lived in both parts of California, in New England, and in the Midwest. I draw on this experience for examples in this chapter. An instructor who has lived in different parts of the world could probably provide better examples. Students—especially those who might be from other cultures—can also be a source of good examples from their experience and often enjoy providing them. Students who belong to ethnic minorities should also be encouraged to describe the ways in which mainstream psychology does or does not apply to themselves and the people they know.

A fair portion of this chapter ventures into the debate between deconstructionism and realism. Deconstructionism is of course a widespread viewpoint in other parts of academia, especially literature departments, but has barely affected psychology. To the extent the instructor or students have expertise in these other areas an interesting and more general discussion of the construction of reality—inside and outside of psychology—might be possible.

Obviously my own position on this issue is that of a realist. An instructor who disagrees on this point could construct an interesting and useful lecture about how and why he or she disagrees.

The chapter discusses the debate over abortion rights in the context of contrasting the individualist and collectivist viewpoint. This is hazardous material, of course; some students will find it emotionally involving. A class debate on this subject might easily generate more heat than light, and I am not sure I would recommend

it. The comments in the text are meant to be neutral and designed to point out only why reasonable compromise is so difficult.

Finally, I would urge instructors of this material to underscore for their students the phenomenological theme that ties together Chapters 14 and 15. It is one's experience of the world that is all-important, and to understand other people we must understand their points of view even if—especially if—they are very different from our own.

## Reader Notes

All the selections in Part VI of the Reader are directly relevant to this chapter. The Reader includes two cross-cultural investigations of personality, one by the anthropologist Caughey and the other by the psychologists Yang and Bond. It also includes an argument for the importance of cultural differences within national boundaries, by Jones and Thorne. The Reader includes an excerpt from the article by Markus and Kitayama discussed in this chapter, and a brief exposition of the deconstructionist view of self taken from a popular novel (by Lodge). The Reader ends with Triandis's major theoretical paper, which presents the three dimensions of cultural variation summarized in this chapter.

## Discussion Questions

1. *Have you ever lived in a different culture, or known well someone from a different culture? Do*

people in that other culture view things *differently? How fundamental are these differences?*

2. *If you wanted to really understand another culture, such as one on an island in the South Pacific, what would you have to do? How could you be sure your interpretation of that culture was correct?*

3. *Have you encountered the concept of deconstructionism in other courses or in your reading? How was it presented in that other context? What do you think about it?*

4. *What are the pros and cons of living in an individualist versus a collectivist culture? Which do you think you would prefer? Is your preference a result of your own cultural conditioning?*

5. *What do you think is more important: The differences between cultures, or the differences among individuals within cultures?*

6. *Consider the example, presented in the text, of the practice of female genital mutilation. Can we judge this practice as wrong? On what grounds—if any—can we judge the practices of another culture as moral or immoral?*

## *Multiple-Choice Questions*

1. Your text suggests that cross-cultural differences in experience, personality, and behavior essentially reflect
   a. different cultural construals of reality.

   b. varying degrees of psychological adjustment across cultures.
   c. maladaptive parenting styles in non-Western cultures.
   d. deconstructionist tendencies in collectivist cultures.

   Answer: a    Page: 308
   Topic: Cultural Variations in Experience, Personality, & Behavior

2. Psychologists who are concerned that the results of contemporary empirical research may not apply to all of humanity are questioning the _____ of those results.
   a. reliability
   b. generalizability
   c. cross-cultural flexibility
   d. construct validity

   Answer: b    Page: 309
   Topic: The Importance of Cross-Cultural Differences

3. It has been suggested that the only real way that psychologists can address the generalizability issue is to
   a. conduct research using subjects from around the world.
   b. limit their focus to one homogeneous sample at a time.
   c. subtract the effects of culture from their research findings.
   d. repeat their studies in carefully controlled laboratory settings.

   Answer: a    Page: 309

Topic: The Importance of Cross-Cultural Differences

4. It is important to identify cross-cultural differences in experience, personality, and behavior because
   a. the differences, if not understood, may cause misunderstandings.
   b. such differences tell us about the variability in human experience.
   c. cross-cultural research informs us about the generalizability of research findings.
   d. all of the above

   Answer: d   Pages: 309–11
   Topic: The Importance of Cross-Cultural Differences

5. If two cultures experience the same emotions, seek the same goals, and organize their thoughts in comparable ways, then the two cultures
   a. are individualistic cultures.
   b. have collectivist construals.
   c. have "experience near" constructs.
   d. view the world through culture-free lenses.

   Answer: c   Page: 311
   Topic: The Importance of Cross-Cultural Differences

6. Ethnocentrism is the tendency to
   a. see members of groups we don't belong to as all being alike.

   b. judge another culture from the point of view of our own.
   c. see members of our own ethnic group as all being very different from one another.
   d. limit the focus of cross-cultural research by studying one group at a time.

   Answer: b   Page: 312
   Topic: Ethnocentrism

7. We are most likely to commit ethnocentrism when the "real" nature of the situation
   a. is difficult to understand.
   b. directly affects us.
   c. seems very obvious.
   d. does not involve us.

   Answer: c   Page: 312
   Topic: Ethnocentrism

8. An American psychologist is using an assessment device called the Strange Situation to measure the quality of an infant's attachment to its mother. Experience tells hims that American babies who have developed secure attachments usually cry when they are left alone and immediately run to their mother when she returns. However, he has recently found that German babies do not appear upset by Mother's departure and frequently ignore her when she returns. His conclusion that these German babies have not formed secure attachments to their mothers may be colored by
   a. ethnocentrism.
   b. racism.

c. the outgroup homogeneity bias.

d. deconstructionism.

Answer: a    Page: 312–13
Topic: Ethnocentrism

9. The tendency to see members of your own group as being very different from one another but the members of groups you don't belong to as being very similar to each other is called the
a. ethnocentric error.
b. in-group favoritism bias.
c. outgroup homogeneity bias.
d. cultural diversity error.

Answer: c    Page: 313
Topic: Outgroup Bias

10. John thinks that women are pretty much all alike whereas men are quite different from one another. John's beliefs about men and women reflect
a. the outgroup homogeneity bias.
b. an incomplete gender categorization.
c. ethnocentrism.
d. the etics of gender.

Answer: a    Page: 313
Topic: Outgroup Bias

11. "The individualistic society of the Xanus appreciates the fundamental tendency for human beings to develop a unique sense of self and thus allows them to develop an advanced type of self esteem that is not possible in the less-advanced collectivist cultures." This statement would most likely be made by a researcher who
a. adopted a deconstructivist point of view.
b. had "gone native" and romanticized the culture being studied.
c. conducted "research by 747."
d. had conducted an idiographic assessment.

Answer: b    Page: 314
Topic: Going Native

12. Among psychologists, the most common approach to cross-cultural issues is to
a. adopt idiographic assessment strategies.
b. claim that comparisons are impossible because no common frame of reference exists.
c. compare different cultures along common dimensions.
d. ignore them.

Answer: d    Page: 314
Topic: Ignoring Cross-Cultural Issues

13. The intellectual approach of _____ is the basis of cultural psychology's claim that there is no culture-free way to look at any culture and that all cultural views of reality are equally valid.
a. ethnocentrism
b. deconstructionism
c. ecological realism
d. collectivism

Answer: b   Page: 315
Topic: Deconstructionism

14. The _____ capacity is the human capacity to invent and use symbol systems.
    a. emic
    b. etic
    c. semiotic
    d. artifactual

Answer: c   Page: 316
Topic: Deconstructionism—The Semiotic Subject

15. Cultural psychologists see people as being _____ who do not have traits, mental states, or psychological processes that are independent from culture.
    a. semiotic subjects
    b. emic individuals
    c. culture-free collectivists
    d. individualistic systems

Answer: a   Page: 316
Topic: Deconstructionism—The Semiotic Subject

16. The deconstructionist approach to cultural psychology claims that
    a. psychological processes are universal.
    b. cultures should be compared on common dimensions.
    c. each culture must be examined in its own terms.
    d. idiographic assessments are the only culture-free method of studying groups.

Answer: c   Page: 316

Topic: Deconstructionism—The Semiotic Subject

17. Shweder and Bourne (1982) asked Hindu and American informants to describe people they knew. The Americans tended to use trait terms like "He is kind" about fifty percent of the time, while the Hindus were more likely to use descriptive contextualized phrases like "He has trouble giving things to his family." How would deconstructionist cultural psychologists interpret these findings?
    a. The idea that people possess personality traits is likely an arbitrary social construction.
    b. Hindus do not have conceptions of each others' personality traits.
    c. Both Americans and Hindus understand the concept of traits but may differ in how they use trait terms.
    d. both a and b

Answer: d   Pages: 316–17
Topic: Deconstructionism—The Indian Sense of Self

18. The point that cultures cannot be compared or classified on common dimensions because those dimensions may not be relevant to all cultures resembles Allport's argument in favor of
    a. idiographic assessment of individuals.
    b. development of culture-free tests.
    c. nomothetic assessment of people.

d. semiotic analysis of groups.

Answer: a   Page: 319
Topic: Deconstructionism—On
   Categorization

19. According to one view, one of
the most devastating difficulties
with a deconstructionist approach
to studying cultural variation is
that it
a. comes very close to making
   cross-cultural psychology impossible.
b. focuses too much on comparisons across different cultures.
c. does not allow researchers to
   understand cultures in their
   own terms.
d. all of the above

Answer: a   Page: 319
Topic: Deconstructionism—On
   Categorization

20. The _____ ap-
proach to research on cultural
variation involves classifying
cultures along common dimensions and studying their similarities and differences.
a. deconstructionist cultural
b. comparative cultural
c. collectivist
d. structural

Answer: b   Page: 320
Topic: The Comparative Cultural Approach

21. Components of ideas that are
particular to a specific culture are
called _____ and

components that are universal
across cultures are called
_____.
a. individualisms; collectivisms
b. emics; etics
c. cultures; values
d. etics; emics

Answer: b   Page: 320
Topic: Emics and Etics

22. The finding that the Big Five
personality factors can be identified cross-culturally if one allows
for some variation of the specific
traits that make up each of the
Big Five is closely related to the
idea(s) of _____
in the comparative cultural approach.
a. deconstructionism
b. collectivism vs. individualism
c. tightness vs. looseness
d. emics and etics

Answer: d   Page: 320
Topic: Emics and Etics

23. Triandis has proposed that cultures vary along which of the
following dimensions?
a. tightness vs. looseness
b. complexity
c. individualism and collectivism
d. all of the above

Answer: d   Page: 320
Topic: Differences Among Cultures

24. If less than two percent of a
country's population exhibited
left-handedness, then Triandis

would say that the culture was likely

a. a tight culture.
b. a simple culture.
c. a collectivist culture.
d. an easy culture.

Answer: a   Page: 323
Topic: Differences Among Cultures.

25. Research indicates that people in _____ cultures tend to strictly observe social hierarchies while those in _____ cultures are less attentive to differences in status.
a. tight; loose
b. collectivist; individualistic
c. simple; complex
d. tough; easy

Answer: b   Page: 324
Topic: Differences Among Cultures

26. Research comparing individualistic and collectivist cultures has found that in individualistic cultures people are more likely to
a. emphasize obligations, reciprocity, and duty to others.
b. be right-handed.
c. marry for love.
d. be ethnically homogeneous.

Answer: c   Page: 325
Topic: Differences Among Cultures

27. Cultural tightness is analogous to the personality traits of
a. idiocentrism and allocentrism.

b. conscientiousness and intolerance for ambiguity.
c. extraversion and introversion.
d. neuroticism and emotional stability.

Answer: b   Page: 326
Topic: Differences Among Cultures

28. In Triandis' model, the distinctive tasks a culture has needed to accomplish and the physical layout and resources of their land is called the culture's
a. ecology.
b. complexity.
c. socialization processes.
d. personality.

Answer: a   Page: 327–28
Topic: The Ecological Approach

29. Differences in ecology can result in differences in the
a. personality of the area's inhabitants.
b. tightness vs. looseness of the culture.
c. collectivism or individualism of the culture.
d. all of the above

Answer: d   Page: 328
Topic: The Ecological Approach

30. The view in cross-cultural psychology that variations between cultures are more important than variations between people within a culture is a _____ view.
a. collectivist

b. individualistic
c. ecological
d. relativist

Answer: a     Page: 329
Topic:  Implications of Cultural
    Psychology

31. Psychologists frequently assume
    that while there may be consider-
    able variation in _____
    across culture, gender, social
    class, and ethnic group,
    _____ can be considered
    universal.
    a. process; content
    b. content; process
    c. attitudes; values
    d. values; attitudes

Answer: b     Page: 330
Topic:  Implications of Cultural
    Psychology

32. One existential view is that the
    universal human condition is the
    need to
    a. exist, work, relate to others,
       and die.
    b. develop a sense of self and
       conditions of worth.
    c. think, feel, and behave.
    d. pursue "personal projects."

Answer: a     Pages: 331
Topic:  The Implications of Cul-
    tural Psychology

16

# How the World Creates Who You Are: Behaviorism and the View from Outside

## Summary

Behaviorism's key tenet is that we can only know about what we can see, and we can see everything we need to know. This translates into a basic belief that all of behavior is a function of the rewards and punishments in one's past and present environment, and how behavior is a function of the environment can be seen through a functional analysis. The philosophical roots of behaviorism include empiricism, a belief that all knowledge comes from experience; associationism, a belief that two stimuli paired together will come to be seen as one; hedonism, the belief that the goal of life is gentle pleasure; and utilitarianism, the belief that the best society is the social arrangement that creates the most happiness for the most people. In behaviorist terminology, learning is any change in behavior that results from experience. Basic principles of learning include habituation, classical conditioning, and operant conditioning. Classical conditioning affects emotions and feelings; operant conditioning affects behavior. Key figures in the development of operant conditioning include Edward Thorndike, Clark Hull, and B. F. Skinner. Punishment is a useful technique of operant conditioning if it is applied correctly, which it almost never is. Behaviorism has contributed a useful technology of behavioral change, and forced the rest of the field to clarify and defend its use of mentalistic concepts (such as thought and mind). But behaviorism neglects important topics such as motivation, emotion, and cognition.

## About the Chapter

Much of this chapter is a review of basic principles of classical and operant conditioning that most students should have learned earlier—and perhaps remembered—from their introductory psychology course. The only distinctive point made here is my claim that classical conditioning better explains emotions, and operant conditioning better explains behavior. The chapter also contains a detailed presentation on how to punish correctly, included because I think it contains some useful advice for future parents and managers from a behavioral perspective.

## Teaching Notes

Because much of this material should at least sound familiar to students, they should not find it difficult. If students are unfamiliar with basic behavioral principles (such as extinction, schedules of reinforcement, and so on) then their summary in this chapter is probably inadequate and will need to be augmented in lecture.

## Reader Notes

Part VII of the Reader includes material from this and the next two chapters, and is designed to show the progression of thought from behaviorism to social learning theory to the modern cognitive approaches. For this chapter, the first two selections in Part VII (both by Skinner) are directly relevant.

## Discussion Questions

1. *Does all knowledge come from experience? Where else could it come from?*
2. *Why do people do anything? What makes a reward rewarding and a punishment punishing?*
3. *What do you think about the behaviorist idea that it is enough for psychology to be able to predict and to control behavior, and that it is unnecessary (and impossible) to know about what goes on inside the mind? Does psychology need to address the*

*inner workings of the mind?
Why or why not?*

4. *Consider the text's discussion of punishment. Do you think punishment is too dangerous to use at all? Given the difficulties, when—if ever—is its use appropriate?*

## Multiple-Choice Questions

1. Behaviorists believe that all of the important causes of behavior can be found in an individual's
   a. unconscious mind.
   b. conscious mind.
   c. personality traits.
   d. environment.

   Answer: d   Page: 337
   Topic: How the World Creates
       Who You Are

2. Behaviorists assert that personality and all of its causes can be directly observed by looking at a person's
   a. environment.
   b. conscious mind.
   c. behavior.
   d. both a and c

   Answer: d   Page: 338
   Topic: How the World Creates
       Who You Are

3. The behaviorists' attempt to determine how behavior is connected to the environment is called
   a. functional analysis.
   b. empiricism.
   c. associationism.

   d. behavioral linking.

   Answer: a   Page: 338
   Topic: Functional Analysis

4. According to behaviorism, what is the connector between the stimuli of the environment and the person's behavior?
   a. cognition
   b. learning
   c. motivation
   d. affect

   Answer: b   Page: 338
   Topic: Functional Analysis

5. Behaviorism has its philosophical roots in
   a. associationism.
   b. empiricism.
   c. hedonism.
   d. all of the above

   Answer: d   Page: 339
   Topic: The Philosophical Roots
       of Behaviorism

6. The basic idea behind empiricism is
   a. two things become linked mentally if they are experienced close together in time.
   b. the structure of the mind determines our experience of reality.
   c. everything we know is the result of our experience with reality.
   d. every large phenomenon can be understood by breaking it down into smaller components.

Answer: c   Page: 339
Topic: The Philosophical Roots
  of Behaviorism—Empiricism

7. John Locke's conception of the
   newborn mind as a *tabula rasa* is
   closely associated with the idea
   of
   a. associationism.
   b. empiricism.
   c. rationalism.
   d. reductionism.

Answer: b   Page: 339
Topic: The Philosophical Roots
  of Behaviorism—Empiricism

8. If a particular song frequently
   precedes being touched by your
   significant other, then eventually
   hearing the song will make you
   think of being touched by him or
   her. This is the basic idea behind
   a. reductionism.
   b. habituation.
   c. associationism.
   d. hedonism.

Answer: c   Page: 339
Topic: The Philosophical Roots
  of Behaviorism—
  Associationism

9. The idea that personality could
   be best understood if you could
   break it down into specific neural
   mechanisms and discrete biological processes is linked to
   a. associationism.
   b. reductionism.
   c. utilitarianism.
   d. functional analysis.

Answer: b   Page: 341
Topic: The Philosophical Roots
  of Behaviorism—
  Associationism

10. Hedonism provides the
    _____ necessary
    for learning and behavior to oc-
    cur.
    a. motivation
    b. cognition
    c. emotion
    d. knowledge

Answer: a   Page: 341
Topic: The Philosophical Roots
  of Behaviorism—Hedonism

11. When the new mobile is first
    hung over her crib, baby Jessica
    looks at it frequently. After sev-
    eral weeks pass, she spends
    hardly any time looking at the
    mobile. Jessica has become
    _____ to the
    mobile.
    a. classically conditioned
    b. operantly conditioned
    c. habituated
    d. counterconditioned

Answer: c   Page: 343
Topic: Three Kinds of Learning—Habituation

12. In Pavlov's famous studies, when
    presentation of meat was fre-
    quently preceded by the sound of
    a bell, the dogs
    a. refused to eat the meat.
    b. began to salivate to the sound
       of the bell.
    c. showed fear responses to the
       bell.

d. salivated only when actually given the meat.

Answer: b   Page: 344–45
Topic: Three Kinds of Learning—Classical Conditioning

13. Pavlov's experiments on the timing of associations demonstrated that two things become associated because
   a. one concept is simply attached to another concept.
   b. the UCS always precedes the CS.
   c. one concept changes the meaning of the other concept.
   d. physical responses can only be elicited by physical stimuli.

Answer: c   Page: 345
Topic: Three Kinds of Learning—Classical Conditioning

14. If the CS fails to be followed by the UCS many times, the organism will experience
   a. extinction.
   b. habituation.
   c. stimulus generalization.
   d. counterconditioning.

Answer: a   Page: 346
Topic: Three Kinds of Learning—Classical Conditioning

15. As an adult, Jenny loves rocking chairs. She likes sitting in them, buying them, and just looking at them. Her emotional reaction to rocking chairs is most likely attributable to
   a. second-order conditioning.

b. habituation.
c. counter-conditioning.
d. operant conditioning.

Answer: a   Page: 346
Topic: Three Kinds of Learning—Classical Conditioning

16. Which of the following cannot be classically conditioned?
   a. eye blinks
   b. claustrophobia
   c. insulin release by the pancreas
   d. None of the above. All can be classically conditioned.

Answer: d   Pages: 346–47
Topic: Three Kinds of Learning—Classical Conditioning

17. It has been suggested that chronic anxiety is the result of
   a. pairing a primary reinforcer with a punisher.
   b. the law of effect.
   c. repeated exposure to stimuli that are unpredictable and random.
   d. second-order conditioning and stimulus generalization.

Answer: c   Page: 347
Topic: Three Kinds of Learning—Classical Conditioning

18. Thorndike's Law of Effect is
   a. a response will be strengthened if it is paired with a desirable outcome.
   b. an organism will stop responding if an conditioned stimulus fails to be followed

by the unconditioned stimulus.

c. stimuli that are similar to the conditioned stimulus will elicit the same response.

d. behaviors that have many effects be more likely to be incorporated into an organism's personality.

Answer: a   Page: 349
Topic: Three Kinds of Learning—Operant Conditioning

19. A major difference between the ideas of Hull and Thorndike is that, unlike Thorndike, Hull thought that
a. behavior was a function of events in the environment.
b. learning should be conceived of in terms of stimuli and response linkings.
c. behavior was a function of the properties of the organism.
d. the Law of Effect was very similar to classical conditioning.

Answer: c   Page: 350
Topic: Three Kinds of Learning—Operant Conditioning

20. Skinner was one of the first to insist that classical conditioning and operant conditioning
a. function through the same mechanisms.
b. both explain all forms of learning equally well.
c. are different types of learning.
d. both a and b

Answer: c   Page: 351

Topic: Three Kinds of Learning—Operant Conditioning

21. Behavior that acts on the environment and changes it to the organism's advantage is _____ behavior.
a. respondent
b. reinforced
c. operant
d. shaping

Answer: c   Page: 351
Topic: Three Kinds of Learning—Operant Conditioning

22. A light goes on in a room just before an excruciatingly loud buzzer sounds. A subject who startles when the light goes on shows _____ behavior but one who leaves the room to avoid the noise exhibits _____ behavior.
a. respondent; operant
b. operant; respondent
c. conditioned; counterconditioned
d. counterconditioned; conditioned

Answer: a   Page: 351
Topic: Three Kinds of Learning—Operant Conditioning

23. On the first day of kindergarten, Terry's teacher responds to the students every time they ask her a question. By the end of the first week, the teacher will only respond to students who are sitting quietly at their desks. At the end of the second week, the teacher will only respond to students'

questions if they are quietly seated, raise their hand, and wait to be called on before asking their question. Terry's teacher is using _____ to change the students' behavior.
a. habituation
b. shaping
c. punishment
d. secondary conditioning

Answer: b   Pages: 352–53
Topic: Three Kinds of Learning—Operant Conditioning

24. It has been suggested that _____ is better for explaining aspects of personality that are behaviorally based while _____ is better for explaining those that are emotionally based.
a. habituation; operant conditioning
b. classical conditioning; social learning theory
c. associationism; the Law of Effect
d. operant conditioning; classical conditioning

Answer: d   Pages: 354–56
Topic: Classical and Operant Conditioning Compared

25. Punishment involves
a. removing an aversive stimulus in order to increase the frequency of a behavior.
b. introducing an aversive consequence in order to decrease the frequency of a behavior.
c. reinforcing incompatible behavioral responses.

d. both a and b

Answer: b   Page: 357
Topic: Punishment

26. Perhaps the biggest problem associated with the use of punishment is that
a. behaviorists have not been able to identify consequences that are generally punishing.
b. it is almost always administered incorrectly.
c. alternatives to punishment are seldom available.
d. punishing only the specific behavior does not appear to reduce the frequency of that behavior.

Answer: b   Page: 357
Topic: Punishment

27. It has been suggested that the most effective way to decrease the frequency of an undesirable behavior is to
a. reinforce the undesirable behavior.
b. punish the undesirable behavior.
c. reward an incompatible behavior.
d. avoid using secondary punishing stimuli.

Answer: c   Page: 357
Topic: How to Punish

28. One danger associated with the use of punishment is that

a. it is difficult for the punisher to gauge the severity of the punishment.
b. punishment motivates concealment of behavior and avoidance of the punisher.
c. punishment teaches about power differentials.
d. All of the above are dangers.

Answer: d   Page: 359
Topic: Dangers of Punishment

29. A parent who relies on punishment to correct his or her child's behavior will likely find that the child
a. is well-behaved even when the parent is not around.
b. grows up to be an aggressive adult.

c. avoids them whenever possible.
d. both b and c

Answer: d   Pages: 358–59
Topic: Dangers of Punishment

30. Behaviorism's most important intellectual contribution may be its insistence that
a. psychologists should focus on observable, overt behaviors.
b. the conscious mind determines behavior.
c. emotion is the primary motivator of human behavior.
d. human beings have free will

Answer: a   Pages: 360
Topic: Contributions and Shortcomings of Behaviorism

# Motivation, Thought, and Behavior: The Social Learning Theories

## Summary

Three different social learning theories have been constructed by psychologists trying to extend behaviorism's basic tenets and empirical approach to cover topics that classical behaviorism leaves out. Dollard and Miller's social learning theory explains motivation as the result of primary and secondary drives, aggression as the result of frustration, and psychological conflict as the result of the interplay of motivations to approach and avoid a goal. Dollard and Miller also offer a reinforcement-based explanation of some psychoanalytic defense mechanisms.

Rotter's social learning theory offers an explanation of how people make decisions. His expectancy value theory describes an individual's behavioral potential (tendency to do something) as a function of his or her expectancies, the reinforcement value of the goal, and the particular situation. This theory is presented in the form of a quasi-mathematical formula. Rotter also offers an account of psychological maladjustment and prescriptions for psychotherapy.

Bandura's social learning theory includes a notion of efficacy expectations that closely resembles Rotter's expectancies. Bandura's theory goes beyond Rotter's however, in two important ways. Bandura describes the process of observational learning, in which one learns by watching the behaviors and outcomes of others, and he also describes the process of reciprocal determinism, in which one's actions are determined by a self system that originates in the environment, then changes the environment, which in turn affects the self system.

## *About the Chapter*

Even some psychologists may be surprised to learn—as I was—that the well-known theories by Dollard and Miller, by Rotter, and by Bandura were all originally named social learning theory. All three are extensions of behaviorism, although they pursue their extension in somewhat different directions.

The material in this chapter is important, but social learning theory—of any of these three varieties—no longer seems a very active current topic in personality psychology. Most current investigators in this area seem to have moved on to the cognitive social learning or just cognitive approaches such as the ones described in the next chapter.

## *Teaching Notes*

Of all the material in this text, I find the material included in this chapter to be the most difficult to bring to life for students. Much of this material is at a very high level of abstraction and badly needs the apt example and infusion of common sense. My advice to an instructor would simply be to use as many specific examples in lecture as you can come up with.

The pseudo-mathematical formula by Rotter is worth showing to students—it is also included in the selection by Rotter in the Reader—but students need to be told that the formula should not be taken too seriously. There is no way to plug numbers into it; the formula is little more than a shorthand way of describing Rotter's ideas about the causation of behavior.

## *Reader Notes*

The selections in Part VII of the Reader by Rotter and Bandura pertain directly to material in this chapter. The Rotter article includes more about his behavioral prediction formula. The Bandura article is his classic presentation of the self system in reciprocal determinism.

## Discussion Questions

1. *Do you think it is possible to reconcile psychoanalysis with learning theory, as Dollard and Miller tried to do? Is it a good idea to even try?*
2. *Have you ever had something in the future that you were both looking forward to and dreading? Did your feelings about it change over time in the way Dollard and Miller describe?*
3. *Do you think people just want to lash out when they are frustrated, as described by Dollard and Miller's frustration-aggression hypothesis? Can you think of examples that demonstrate this? How about cases where this did not happen? What does a person's reaction to frustration depend on?*
4. *Do you think Rotter's behavioral prediction formula adds anything over and above a verbal statement of the same ideas? What do you think about efforts to make psychology mathematical in this way?*
5. *Can you think of other ways— beyond those described by Bandura—in which people make their own environments?*
6. *A person is under severe stress because he seems surrounded by angry people both at home and at work. According to Bandura's analysis, what might be going on?*

## Multiple-Choice Questions

1. Unlike social learning theory, behaviorism
   a. views human beings as passive organisms.
   b. ignores observational learning.
   c. ignores motivation and cognition.
   d. all of the above

   Answer: d  Page: 362–63
   Topic: What Behaviorism
      Leaves Out

2. Dollard and Miller's key idea concerns
   a. defense mechanisms.
   b. the habit hierarchy.
   c. behavior potential.
   d. reciprocal determinism.

   Answer: b  Page: 363–64
   Topic: Dollard and Miller's Social Learning Theory

3. A ranked ordering of the behaviors that an individual might do is called a(n)
   a. expectancy value theory.
   b. efficacy expectation list.
   c. habit hierarchy.
   d. behavior potential.

   Answer: c  Page: 364
   Topic: Dollard and Miller's Social Learning Theory

4. Dollard and Miller's social learning theory differs from other

social learning approaches because it attempts to explain
a. traditionally Freudian concepts and phenomena.
b. cognitive processes ignored by behaviorists.
c. the role of expectancy.
d. the acquisition of reinforcement values.

Answer: a   Page: 364
Topic: Dollard and Miller's Social Learning Theory

5. According to Dollard and Miller, a state of psychological tension that feels good when it is reduced is called
a. a behavior potential.
b. a drive.
c. motivation.
d. psychological conflict.

Answer: b   Page: 365
Topic: Motivation and Drives

6. Love, prestige, power, fear, and humiliation are
a. secondary drives.
b. primary reinforcers.
c. primary drives.
d. biological needs.

Answer: a   Page: 365
Topic: Motivation and Drives

7. In order for a reward to be reinforcing and produce behavior change, the reward must
a. increase the expectancy value of the behavior.
b. change the habit hierarchy.
c. satisfy a need.

d. produce physiological tension.

Answer: c   Page: 365
Topic: Motivation and Drives

8. According to Dollard and Miller, _____ provides the motivating force for human behavior.
a. expectancy
b. self-efficacy
c. reinforcement value
d. drive-reduction

Answer: d   Page: 365
Topic: Motivation and Drives

9. If you are frustrated because your co-worker's performance prevented you from getting the end-of-the-year bonus you were expecting, Dollard and Miller would predict that your response would be
a. depression.
b. aggressive behavior.
c. feelings of humiliation.
d. avoidance of the situation.

Answer: b   Page: 366–67
Topic: Frustration and Aggression

10. Research on the drive-reduction function of displacement indicates that if you displace your aggression it
a. will make you feel frustration.
b. will not necessarily reduce the aggressive drive.
c. will typically reduce the aggressive drive.

d. None of the above. The research does not allow you to draw any conclusions.

Answer: b    Page: 367
Topic: Frustration and Aggression

11. As a conflicted goal gets closer, the tendency to _____ goal becomes stronger than the corresponding tendency to _____ goal.
    a. avoid a negative; approach a positive
    b. approach a negative; approach a positive
    c. approach a negative; avoid a positive
    d. avoid a positive; avoid a negative

Answer: a    Page: 367–68
Topic: Psychological Conflict

12. Dollard and Miller view psychological conflict as the result of
    a. conflict between the id and the superego.
    b. conflict between primary and secondary drives.
    c. habit hierarchy disorder.
    d. approach-avoidance conflict.

Answer: d    Page: 367–68
Topic: Psychological Conflict

13. Defense mechanisms, according to Dollard and Miller, are
    a. internal drive states that cause aggression.
    b. affective mechanisms for coping with stress caused by the approach-avoidance conflict
    c. cognitive behaviors that are negatively reinforced because they remove anxiety.
    d. mechanisms used by the ego to defend against anxiety produced by psychic conflict.

Answer: c    Page: 369
Topic: Psychological Conflict

14. Julian Rotter's social learning theory focuses primarily on
    a. drives.
    b. decision making.
    c. efficacy expectations.
    d. reciprocal determinism.

Answer: b    Page: 370
Topic: Rotter's Social Learning Theory

15. Mark thinks that if he asks for a $50 a week raise, he will definitely get it. He really wants a $75 a week raise and thinks his chances of getting that are about 50-50. Expectancy value theory would predict that Mark will ask for a _____ a week raise and classic behaviorism would predict that he'll ask for a _____ a week raise.
    a. $50; $75
    b. $75; $50
    c. $50; $50
    d. $75; $75

Answer: a    Page: 370
Topic: Expectancy Value Theory of Decision Making

16. The probability that you will perform a behavior in a given situation is called your
    a. expectancy.
    b. behavior potential.
    c. reinforcement value.
    d. efficacy expectation.

    Answer: b  Page: 371
    Topic: Expectancy Value Theory of Decision Making

17. According to Rotter, locus of control is analogous to
    a. self-efficacy.
    b. a specific expectancy.
    c. reinforcement value.
    d. a generalized expectancy.

    Answer: d  Page: 372
    Topic: Expectancy Value Theory of Decision Making

18. Being in a relationship is very important to Brian but is only moderately important to Matthew. Brian and Matthew have different _____
    for being in a relationship.
    a. expectancies
    b. behavior potentials
    c. efficacy expectations
    d. reinforcement values

    Answer: d  Page: 373
    Topic: Expectancy Value Theory of Decision Making

$$BP_{x,\,S1,\,Ra} = f(E_{x,\,Ra,\,S1}\;\&\;RV_{a,\,S1})$$

19. One translation of Rotter's formula (see above) is

    a. "behavior is a function of the relative importance of the situation and the psychological environment."
    b. "at any given moment, your behavior, personality, and the environment reciprocally determine one another."
    c. "what you are likely to do depends upon whether you think you can get something and how badly you want it under the circumstances."
    d. "behavior problems are a function of efficacy expectations and variability in reinforcement histories."

    Answer: c  Page: 374
    Topic: Expectancy Value Theory of Decision Making

20. Jake really wants to have a Ph.D. in botany but seriously doubts that he'll be able to finish and defend his dissertation. According to Rotter, Jake
    a. is experiencing low self-efficacy.
    b. has an internal locus of control.
    c. will probably become frustrated and act aggressively.
    d. will likely experience depression.

    Answer: d  Page: 374
    Topic: Adjustment and Maladjustment

21. In Rotter's expectancy value theory, psychological conflict results from having

a. two or more behaviors with high RVs.
b. an internal locus of control.
c. conflict in approach-avoidance system.
d. expectancies that are higher than your self-efficacy.

Answer: a   Page: 375
Topic: Adjustment and Maladjustment

22. Rotterian psychotherapy focuses on
a. drive-reduction.
b. goal and expectancy clarification.
c. resolving approach-avoidance conflict.
d. changing efficacy expectations.

Answer: b   Page: 376
Topic: Psychotherapy

23. Bandura's concept of efficacy is similar to what Rotter called
a. situational relativism.
b. reinforcement values.
c. expectancies.
d. behavior potential.

Answer: c   Page: 377
Topic: Efficacy Expectations

24. Barbara thinks that Joe will go out on a date with her *if* she can ever get up the courage to ask him. Barbara's perception of the likelihood that Joe will accept reflects her _____, while her doubts about her ability to ask him out reflect her _____.

a. reinforcement value; behavior potential
b. expectancy; efficacy expectation
c. efficacy expectation; expectancy
d. behavior potential; reinforcement value

Answer: b   Page: 377
Topic: Efficacy Expectations

25. Bandura's efficacy expectation is a belief about
a. what the person is capable of doing.
b. what the likely result of a behavior will be.
c. the worth of an outcome.
d. all of the above

Answer: a   Page: 377
Topic: Efficacy Expectations

26. The key target for psychotherapy, according to Bandura, is to
a. change the client's overt behavior.
b. achieve a match between the client's efficacies and capabilities.
c. change the client's reinforcement values.
d. modify the client's habit hierarchy.

Answer: b   Page: 377
Topic: Efficacy Expectations

27. The "Bobo doll" studies of aggression demonstrated that

a. changing efficacy expectations can facilitate behavioral change.
b. expectancies vary across situations.
c. children will imitate positive but not negative behaviors.
d. learning can occur vicariously through observation.

Answer: d    Page: 378
Topic: Observational Learning

28. The element of reciprocal determinism that is the most significant departure from classic behaviorism is the idea that
a. the organism's behavior is a function of the environment.
b. the environment can be changed by an organism's behavior.
c. the self can affect behavior independent of the environment.
d. learning occurs through direct reinforcement for behavior.

Answer: c    Page: 379
Topic: Reciprocal Determinism and the Self

29. As a child, Robin was frequently surrounded by many people and came to see herself as a very so-ciable person. As an adult, Robin has chosen a career that requires her to interact with other people on a daily basis and, as a result, is becoming even more sociable than before. This process is called
a. the approach-avoidance goal system.
b. reciprocal determinism.
c. vicarious learning.
d. the expectancy value theory.

Answer: b    Page: 379
Topic: Reciprocal Determinism and the Self

30. All of the social learning theorists discussed in the text agree that the important causes of behavior
a. are located in the environment.
b. involve an interaction between your mind and the environment.
c. are located in your conscious mind.
d. result from direct reinforcement for the behavior.

Answer: b    Page: 380
Topic: Reciprocal Determinism and the Self

# Cognition and Personality

## Summary

The cognitive approach consists of various attempts to combine recent developments in cognitive psychology with the concerns of personality psychology. Modern cognitive psychology describes the mind as a system for organizing and storing information—memory, in short. A general model of this system was described, in which information passes through the sensory/perceptual buffer into short-term memory, working memory, and long-term memory. Long-term memory includes both declarative and procedural knowledge. Several important modern theorists are extending the terminology and ideas in this model into the domain of personality. Mischel's cognitive social learning theory, and its recent amendment, describes five cognitive person variables and describes the individual differences produced by these variables as patterns of behaviors that vary across situations. Cantor and Kihlstrom describe personality as social intelligence, which comprises everything you know about the world and your skills for using that knowledge. In the terms of social intelligence theory, schemas are mental structures that hold factual knowledge, goals are desired ends that organize and motivate behavior, and strategies are characteristic means of attaining goals. The same goal can be approached through different strategies. Dweck's cognitive approach to motivation distinguishes between two kinds of individual. Entity theorists believe personality attributes and abilities are fixed, desire to prove their competence, and respond to failure with helplessness. Incremental theorists believe attributes and abilities can be changed, desire to improve, and respond to failure with even greater effort. In the final analysis, the cognitive approach is more similar to than different from the trait approach. Even though they use somewhat different terminology, both approaches try to describe patterns of individual differences in behavior and the psychological processes behind them.

## About the Chapter

This chapter begins by tracing how cognitive approaches developed out of social learning theory (especially Bandura's version) that developed from behaviorism. Next, a generic model of how the mind processes information is presented. Along the way, I try to point out where aspects of information processing described in the model are relevant to personality processes. Finally, the chapter presents several modern cognitive perspectives on personality, by Mischel, Cantor and Kihlstrom, and Dweck.

The view I take of the cognitive approach is somewhat skeptical. Much of the research is valuable, but I think it unfortunate that an implicit (sometimes explicit) part of the agenda of the cognitive social learning theorists is to belittle the importance of personality traits. In many cases—such as Dweck's—it is possible to reconceptualize some of their most important concepts as personality traits! More importantly, the cognitive and trait approaches are not as far apart as they might look. In the future I hope these approaches can develop a cooperative rather than habitually antagonistic relationship.

In fact, the great strength of the cognitive approach is its potential to integrate rather than separate some of the divergent approaches within personality psychology. It is already possible to see elements of behaviorism, social learning theory, psychoanalysis, phenomenology, and trait approaches in modern cognitive conceptualizations. That is, many such conceptualizations include reinforcement, expectancies, unconscious processes (see some of Kihlstrom's recent work), the person's interpretation of reality, and individual differences. If these connections become more clearly recognized, the cognitive approach to personality may end up being the one with the greatest potential to integrate all of the others. But that time is still a long way off, and many obstacles must be overcome first.

## Teaching Notes

Students find this material, like that in preceding chapter, rather dry, and so extra efforts are needed to make them see its relevance.

Instructors will vary in how they want to portray the modern cognitive approaches to personality. It is plausible to present it as the wave of the future, as a distraction from the truly interesting issues in personality psychology, or as a rediscovery of the wheel. My own approach is to present it as promising but still in its very early stages of development. My prediction is that it will someday be integrated with trait theory, but which approach will absorb the other remains to be seen.

## Reader Notes

Mischel's original exposition of cognitive social learning theory, Norem's research with optimistic and pessimistic strategies, and Dweck's theory of motivation are all represented in the Reader. All of this is directly relevant to material in this chapter.

## Discussion Questions

1.  *Have you taken a course in cognitive psychology? If so, do you think that approach can be integrated into personality psychology?*
2.  *What do you find more useful for thinking about people: personality trait concepts or concepts such as strategies and plans? Does the preferred concept depend on your purpose?*
3.  *Do you think optimistic and pessimistic strategies work equally well in motivating academic performance? What are some advantages and disadvantages of each strategy? Which one do you use?*
4.  *Do you know any entity or incremental theorists, as described by Dweck? How do they act? What do they do after they fail at something? What do they do after they succeed?*
5.  *What ideas from other approaches can you find in the cognitive approach to personality? Do you think it will someday absorb these other approaches?*

## Multiple-Choice Questions

1. Which of the following has influenced the cognitive approach to personality?
   a. the phenomenological approach
   b. behaviorism
   c. psychoanalysis
   d. all of the above

   Answer: d    Pages: 382–83
   Topic: Roots of the Cognitive Approach

2. The sensory buffer can only hold
   a. about seven chunks of information.
   b. information for less than two or three seconds.
   c. visual information while the original stimulus is still present.
   d. information that has been identified and interpreted by the perceiver.

   Answer: b    Page: 384
   Topic: The Sensory/Perceptual Buffer

3. Research on the cocktail party effect demonstrates that
   a. between five and nine pieces of information can be held in short-term memory.
   b. alcohol consumption interferes with the information transfer between working memory and long-term memory.
   c. information that enters our sensory/perceptual buffer outside of our conscious awareness is being monitored and can be retrieved.
   d. ego defense mechanisms may prevent certain anxiety-provoking stimuli from entering consciousness.

   Answer: c    Pages: 385–86
   Topic: The Sensory/Perceptual Buffer

4. The selective functioning of the sensory/perceptual buffer has been tentatively linked to the psychoanalytic concept(s) of
   a. defense mechanisms.
   b. parapraxes.
   c. the preconscious mind.
   d. sublimation.

   Answer: a    Page: 386
   Topic: The Sensory/Perceptual Buffer

5. The phrase "seven plus or minus two" refers to the
   a. number of seconds information can be held in the perceptual buffer.
   b. capacity of short-term memory.
   c. number of years information can be stored in long-term memory before it is replaced with new information.
   d. organizational structure of schemas.

   Answer: b    Page: 387
   Topic: Short-Term Memory

6. According to research on short-term memory, which of the following could be easily retained in short-term memory?
   a. Twelve single digit numbers (e.g. 1, 9, 6, 2, 4, 2, 5, 9, 3, 0, 7, 7)
   b. Ten first names.
   c. Six phone numbers including area codes.
   d. The names of twenty unrelated but commonly used household products.

   Answer: c   Page: 387
   Topic: Short-Term Memory

7. Short-term memory is roughly equivalent to _____ thought and working memory is similar to _____ thought.
   a. unconscious; subconscious
   b. preconscious; unconscious
   c. subconscious; conscious
   d. conscious; preconscious

   Answer: d   Pages: 388
   Topic: Short-Term Memory

8. As a person becomes an expert in an area, they will begin to _____ to help them organize the information.
   a. use larger chunks
   b. develop more elaborate schemas
   c. use smaller chunks
   d. both a and b

   Answer: d   Pages: 388, 402
   Topic: Short-Term Memory

9. This morning you noticed that you needed some things from the grocery store. While at the store, you will use _____ memory to recall those items into consciousness.
   a. declarative
   b. procedural
   c. working
   d. short-term

   Answer: c   Page: 389
   Topic: Working Memory

10. Research indicates that the most effective way to commit information to long-term memory is to
    a. repeat the information over and over again.
    b. limit your attention to about seven specific pieces of information.
    c. ask yourself, "How does this information apply to me?"
    d. All of the above are equally effective.

    Answer: c   Page: 390
    Topic: From Short-Term to Long-Term Memory

11. The consensus of modern cognitive psychologists is that the storage capacity of long term memory is
    a. essentially limitless.
    b. limited to about seven chunks of information.
    c. decreases with age.
    d. increases with age.

    Answer: a   Page: 391
    Topic: Long-Term Memory

12. If you know that Freud used the technique of free association in psychotherapy you have _____ about free association. If you know how to use the technique of free association yourself, you have _____.
    a. long-term storage; working memory
    b. perceptual knowledge; sensory knowledge
    c. declarative knowledge; procedural knowledge
    d. event memory; conceptual memory

Answer: c   Pages: 391–94
Topic: Long-Term Memory

13. _____ memory contains your general knowledge of the world and an understanding of how it works.
    a. Conceptual
    b. Event
    c. Procedural
    d. Working

Answer: a   Page: 392
Topic: Long-Term Memory

14. Your expectations about sequences of events that should occur in certain situations are called cognitive
    a. schemas.
    b. expectancies.
    c. scripts.
    d. heuristics.

Answer: c   Page: 392
Topic: Long-Term Memory

15. On Jason's first visit to a psychologist, he was surprised to find that his psychologist did not resemble Freud in either looks or behavior and didn't ask him to lay on a couch and recite his dreams. Jason's trip to the psychologist did not match his _____ about psychologists and therapy sessions.
    a. cognitive and behavioral constructions
    b. procedural and declarative knowledge
    c. encoding strategies and personal constructs
    d. stereotypes and scripts

Answer: d   Page: 392–93
Topic: Long-Term Memory

16. Knowing how to swim, act charming, and tell a joke are generally learned by acquiring _____ knowledge.
    a. conceptual
    b. procedural
    c. declarative
    d. event

Answer: b   Page: 394
Topic: Long-Term Memory

17. Your art teacher is trying to help you improve your painting techniques. She encourages you to just choose a subject and begin painting and later gives you feedback on your completed painting. Your art teacher is attempting to teach
    a. subjective stimulus values.
    b. procedural knowledge.
    c. encoding strategies.

d. construction competencies.

Answer: b    Page: 395
Topic: Long-Term Memory

18. Emotions are a separate category of
a. encoding strategies.
b. subjective stimulus values.
c. procedural knowledge.
d. declarative memories.

Answer: c    Page: 396
Topic: Long-Term Memory

19. According to Mischel,
_____ com-
prise a person's intelligence, social skills, and creativity.
a. encoding strategies and personal constructs
b. subjective stimulus values
c. self-regulatory systems
d. cognitive and behavioral construction competencies

Answer: d    Pages: 397
Topic: Cognitive Person Variables

20. In Mischel's theory, the person
variables of _____
correspond to Bandura's self
system and _____
correspond to Rotter's notion of
expectancies.
a. self-regulatory systems and
plans; subjective stimulus
values
b. encoding strategies and personal constructs; subjective
stimulus values

c. behavioral construction competencies; cognitive competencies
d. personal constructs; plans

Answer: a    Pages: 397–98
Topic: Cognitive Person Variables

21. The latest version of Mischel's
theory claims the most important
aspect of the social learning
cognitive variables is
a. their influence on personality
traits.
b. the way in which they simul-
taneously interact.
c. the reciprocal determinism
between thought and behavior.
d. that they create an approach
to personality that integrates
the trait and cognitive perspectives.

Answer: b    Page: 399
Topic: The Personality System

22. Mischel views personality variables as _____
while trait psychologists consider
them to be _____.
a. mental processes; patterns of
actions
b. emotional variability; behavioral consistencies
c. cognitively based; affectively
based.
d. strategies; goals

Answer: a    Page: 400
Topic: Cognitive vs. Trait Approaches

23. Mischel's claim that his theory avoids trait concepts has been criticized because
    a. encoding strategies are essentially manifestations of locus of control.
    b. his latest theory allows for the influence of temperament.
    c. if you factor analyze his person variables, the Big Five emerges.
    d. he moves personality from something you have to something you do.

    Answer: b   Pages: 400–1
    Topic: Cognitive vs. Trait Approaches

24. The mental structure of everything you know about yourself is your
    a. self-efficacy.
    b. self-regulatory system.
    c. personal construct.
    d. self-schema.

    Answer: d   Page: 402
    Topic: Schemas

25. Paul thinks that he is very intelligent and is aware of the various ways he has demonstrated his intelligence in numerous situations. He interprets his every action and every situation he enters in terms of its relevance to his intelligence. Paul has
    a. a cognitive script for intelligence.
    b. an elaborate self-schema for intelligence.
    c. constructed an intelligent possible self.

    d. selected intelligence as his current concern.

    Answer: b   Page: 402
    Topic: Schemas

26. In Cantor and Kihlstrom's conceptualization of schemas, a person can change their self-schema by
    a. experiencing a serious trauma.
    b. imagining a possible self to strive for.
    c. experiencing doubt about the world.
    d. all of the above

    Answer: d   Pages: 402–3
    Topic: Schemas

27. General goals serve to
    a. motivate specific behaviors.
    b. organize daily activities.
    c. provide a clear purpose in life.
    d. all of the above

    Answer: d   Page: 403
    Topic: Goals

28. One view of goals is that it is most advantageous to have the ability to
    a. develop primarily general, long-term goals.
    b. shift between short- and long-term goals.
    c. formulate very specific goals.
    d. set general goals that are separate from your daily activities.

    Answer: b   Page: 403
    Topic: Goals

29. Research by Julie Norem indicates that defensive pessimists and eternal optimists likely
    a. use different strategies but obtain similar ends.
    b. have similar specific goals but different general goals.
    c. use the same strategies but obtain different ends.
    d. have different learning goals but similar performance goals.

    Answer: a   Page: 404
    Topic: Strategies

30. A _____ goal is one in which the individual is interested in increasing his or her competence and a _____ goal is one in which the individual is concerned with gaining favorable judgments of his or her competence.
    a. general; specific
    b. performance; learning
    c. specific; general
    d. learning; performance

    Answer: d   Page: 405
    Topic: Performance and Learning Goals

31. A person with an incremental theory of ability will respond to failure with a _____ pattern of behavior.
    a. helpless
    b. mastery-oriented
    c. anxiety-driven

    d. defensively pessimistic
    Answer: b   Page: 405
    Topic: Performance and Learning Goals

32. Sharon believes that intelligence and ability are something that you are just born with and you can't do anything to change them. Sharon has a(n) _____ theory of ability.
    a. entity
    b. incremental
    c. schematic
    d. cognitive

    Answer: a   Page: 406
    Topic: Performance and Learning Goals

33. Which of the following is a similarity between the cognitive approach and the modern trait approach to personality?
    a. Both attempt to identify processes that create individual differences in behavior.
    b. Both attempt to identify the genetic and experiential origins of individual differences.
    c. Both a and b are similarities.
    d. Neither a nor b. Cognitive and trait approaches have no similarities.

    Answer: c   Pages: 408–9
    Topic: The Cognitive Approach and Its Intersections

# Looking Back and Looking Ahead

## Summary

Each of the different approaches to personality psychology has aspects of the person it explains rather well, and other aspects it does not explain or ignores entirely. Thus, the choice between them depends not upon which one is right, but what one wishes to know. To make progress as a personality psychologist it is probably necessary to choose one of these approaches, but one should try to stay open to alternative approaches when necessary. The future of personality psychology may include further development of the cognitive approach, renewed attention to emotion and experience, progress in biology and better understanding of its limits, a reconceptualization of cross-cultural approaches, and an increased integration of personality, social, and cognitive psychology. In the end, personality psychology is an attempt to turn our observations of each other into mutual understanding.

## About the Chapter

This chapter provides a brief overview of the principal approaches to personality covered in the preceding chapters. It reiterates the main point of the book, that the different approaches are not different answers to the same question, but different questions. I consider the prospects for integrating the approaches, but reach the conclusion that they address issues that are different enough that all will probably survive indefinitely in some form. I make a case that it is often if not always better to keep these approaches and their questions separate than to mix them together, and reveal my own true colors as a trait theorist. It is unlikely any reader will be surprised.

## Teaching Notes

Now is the time for an instructor to make all those overview and comparative comments that he or she was tempted to provide to students on the first day of the term. If you have a favorite approach, this is a good time to make a pitch for it. If you disagree with my organization of or definition of the basic approaches, this is a good time to explain your own preferred system to your students. In general, this is a good time to come clean about your own biases. I reveal—no surprise—that I am a trait theorist, and I would urge an instructor to reveal his or her own favorite approach to students, and explain why.

This point in the course also offers one last chance to convince students that personality psychology is meaningful and important. Consider this: Soon, your students will be voting for college construction bonds and representatives who determine the budgets of agencies that award research grants. What do you want them to think about psychology?

## Reader Notes

The final selection in the Reader, included as an Afterword, is a presentation of my own theoretical approach to personality traits.

## Discussion Questions

1. *Is personality psychology really a science? Does the answer to this question matter?*
2. *What is your favorite approach to personality of those covered? What is your least favorite approach? Why?*
3. *Do you think the different approaches to personality will someday be combined into one, integrated approach? Should they be?*
4. *Is personality psychology relevant to:*
   a. *your own daily life?*
   b. *understanding and solving social problems?*
   c. *understanding human nature?*
5. *What do we know when we know a person?*

## Multiple-Choice Questions

1. The _____ approach focuses on our moment to moment conscious experience, free will, and ability to choose reality.
   a. trait
   b. cognitive
   c. humanistic
   d. all of the above

   Answer: c   Page: 411
   Topic: The Different Approaches

2. Each personality paradigm effectively addresses its own key concerns
   a. and has corresponding therapeutic interventions that will change behavior.
   b. as well as the concerns of the other paradigms.
   c. and attempts to explain the functioning of the unconscious.
   d. but tends to ignore pretty much everything else.

   Answer: d   Page: 411
   Topic: The Different Approaches

3. One view of the different personality approaches is that each
   a. is addressing the same basic questions as the other approaches.
   b. addresses fundamentally different questions.
   c. leaves something out.
   d. both b and c

   Answer: d   Page: 412
   Topic: Which One Is Right?

4. According to the text, you should judge a personality approach by which of the following criteria?
   a. correctness
   b. ability to explain unconscious processes
   c. usefulness
   d. ability to integrate affective and cognitive mechanisms

   Answer: c   Page: 412
   Topic: Which One Is Right?

5. If psychologists settled on a single, unifying theory of personality it would likely
   a. result in a theory that is confusing and incoherent.
   b. encourage exploration of diverse phenomena.
   c. stimulate theorizing.
   d. prevent dogmatism.

   Answer: a   Page: 415
   Topic: No Single Perspective Accounts for Everything

6. One prediction about the likely result of blending the strengths and weaknesses of all the different approaches to personality is that it would
   a. give us an understanding of conscious processes but only a rudimentary understanding of the unconscious.
   b. remove exactly what was interesting about each approach.
   c. result in the development of a single, unifying theory of personality.

d. provide a theory that would satisfy behaviorists but not phenomenologists.

Answer: b    Page: 415
Topic:  You Probably Must Choose

7. One prediction about the future of the cognitive approach is that it will
   a. be rejected as unscientific.
   b. focus almost exclusively on determining memory capacity.
   c. examine how information processing affects interpersonal behavior.
   d. circumvent the need to include emotion variables' descriptions of personality systems.

Answer: c    Page: 417
Topic:  Further Developments of the Cognitive Approach

8. In the future, one view is that biological approaches to personality will
   a. identify a specific brain structure that determines personality.
   b. recognize that personality is not linked to genetics.
   c. focus on how biological processes affect personality.
   d. become unnecessary for understanding personality.

Answer: c    Page: 418
Topic:  Biology

9. It has been suggested that the future challenge of cross-cultural psychology will be to
   a. recognize that cross-cultural comparisons are just not possible.
   b. identify constructs that are general enough to allow cross-cultural comparisons.
   c. see each culture in its own terms.
   d. both a and c

Answer: b    Page: 419
Topic:  Cross-Cultural Psychology

10. Current research on the accuracy of personality judgments is an example of
    a. how personality, social, and cognitive psychology can be integrated.
    b. the future direction of biological approaches to personality.
    c. a research paradigm that will not exist in the future.
    d. an integration of psychoanalytic and behavioral approaches to personality.

Answer: a    Page: 419
Topic:  Integration of Personality, Social, and Cognitive Psychology

11. The only way to determine if your understanding of a person's personality is correct is to
    a. determine if it can account for everything about the person.
    b. try to use it to explain or predict what the person does.

c. use it to uncover their unconscious motivations.
d. None of the above. There is
   no way to determine if it is
   correct.

Answer: b    Page: 420
Topic: Integration of Personal-
   ity, Social, and Cognitive
   Psychology